| DATE DUE | | | |
|---|---|---|---|
| | | | |
| | | | |
| | | | |
| | | | |
| | | | |
| | | | |
| | | | |
| | | | |
| | | | |
| | | | |
| | | | |
| | | | |

**CAJO22228**

**202**
**N**

**Nardo, Don.**

**Heroes**

**CANANDAIGUA MIDDLE SCHOOL**
**CANANDAIGUA, NEW YORK 14424**

233807 02196        38134C        006

# Heroes

**Other titles in Lucent Books
Discovering Mythology series include:**

Death and the Underworld
Gods and Goddesses
Monsters
Quests and Journeys

# Heroes

## Discovering Mythology

**Don Nardo**

Lucent Books, Inc.
P.O. Box 289011, San Diego, California

Library of Congress Cataloging-in-Publication Data

Nardo, Don, 1947–
  Heroes / by Don Nardo.
      p. cm. — (Discovering mythology)
  Includes bibliographical references and index.
  Summary: Discusses heroes in the mythology of various cultures, including
  Mesopotamia, Greece, Rome, China, and Native America.
   ISBN 1-56006-851-5 (hardcover : alk. paper)
   1. Heroes—Mythology—Juvenile literature. [1. Heroes. 2. Mythology.] I. Title. II Series.
  BL325.H46 N37 2002
  291.2'13—dc21

                                                                    2001002546


                    Copyright 2002 by Lucent Books, Inc.
            P.O. Box 289011, San Diego, California 92198-9011

                        Printed in the U.S.A.

# Contents

# Foreword

Created by ancient cultures, the world's many and varied mythologies are humanity's attempt to make sense of otherwise inexplicable phenomena. Floods, drought, death, creation, evil, even the possession of knowledge—all have been explained in myth. The ancient Greeks, for example, observed the different seasons but did not understand why they changed. As a result, they reasoned that winter, a cold, dark time of year, was the result of a mother in mourning; the three months of winter were the days the goddess Demeter missed her daughter Persephone who had been tricked into spending part of her year in the underworld. Likewise, the people of India experienced recurring droughts, weeks and months during which their crops withered and their families starved. To explain the droughts, the Indians created the story of Vritra, a terrible demon who lived in the clouds and sucked up all the world's moisture. And the Vikings, in their search for an understanding of wisdom and knowledge, created Odin, their culture's most powerful god, who gave the world the gift of poetry and possessed two mythic ravens named Thought and Memory.

The idea of myth, fantastic stories that answer some of humanity's most enduring questions, spans time, distance, and differing cultural ideologies. Humans—whether living in the jungles of South America, along the rocky coasts of northern Europe, or on the islands of Japan—all formulated stories in an attempt to understand their world. And although their worlds differed greatly, they sometimes found similar ways of explaining the unknown or unexplainable events of their lives. Other times, there were differences, but the method of explanation—the myth—remains the same.

Each book in the Discovering Mythology series revolves around a specific topic—for example, death and the underworld; monsters; or heroes—and each chapter examines a selection of myths related to that topic. This allows young readers to note both the similarities and differences across cultures and time. Almost all cultures have myths to explain creation and death, for instance, but the actual stories sometimes vary widely. The Babylonians believed that the earth was the offspring of primordial parents, while the Navajo Indians of North America assert that the world emerged over time much like an infant grows into an adult. In ancient Greek mythology, a deceased person passed quickly into the underworld, a physical place that offered neither reward nor punishment for one's deeds in life. Egyptian myths, on the other hand, contended that a person's quality of existence in the afterlife, an ambiguous state of being, depended on his actions on earth.

In other cases, the symbolic creature or hero and what it represents are the same, but the purpose of the story may be different. Although monster myths in different cultures may not always explain the same phenomenon or offer insight into the same ethical quandary, monsters nearly always represent evil. The shape-shifting beast-men of ancient Africa represented the evils of trickery and wile. These vicious animal-like creatures transformed themselves into attractive, charming humans to entrap unsuspecting locals. Persia's White Demon devoured townspeople and nobles alike; it took the intelligence and strength of an extraordinary prince to defeat the monster and save the countryside. Even the Greek Furies, although committing their evil acts in the name of justice, were ugly, violent creatures who murdered people guilty of killing others. Only the goddess Athena could tame them.

The Discovering Mythology series presents the myths of many cultures in a format accessible to young readers. Fully documented secondary source quotes and numerous mythological tales enliven the text. Sidebars highlight interesting stories, creatures, and traditions. Annotated bibliographies offer ideas for further research. Each book in this engaging series provides students with a wealth of information as well as launching points for further discussion.

# Halfway Between Gods and Humans

## Introduction

The hero has a thousand faces. This was the way the widely popular lecturer-writer-scholar Joseph Campbell (1904–1987) stated one of the great underlying truths of world mythology. All across the globe and throughout the ages, hundreds of peoples and nations have spawned their individual mythologies, each replete with its own native gods, larger-than-life human figures, and fantastic events. On the surface, the nature and presentation of these mythological elements often vary considerably from one culture to another. The myths of the ancient Greeks and those of the ancient Chinese, for example, might at first glance seem literally worlds apart. Yet as Campbell so shrewdly pointed out, beneath the surface these stories and the characters who act in them have much in common.

The similarities among the myths of the world's cultures are perhaps most obvious and stunning in the image of the hero. All native mythologies feature heroes who perform brave, seemingly impossible deeds, fight monsters and tyrants, discover great secrets or truths, and so forth. The situations and their particulars vary from one culture and story to another; but the basic personal attributes of the hero, as well as the essential elements of his adventure, are almost always the same. Concerning typical heroic attributes, noted classical scholar Michael Grant writes:

> The hero must use his superior qualities at all times to excel and win applause, for that is the reward and demonstration of his manhood. He makes honor his paramount code, and glory the driving force and aim of his existence. Birth, wealth and prowess confirm a hero's title; his ideals are courage, endurance, strength and beauty. Enthusiastically confident in what he achieves and possesses, he relies upon his own ability to make the fullest use of his powers. Yet, although he is no god,

there is something about him which brings him not too far from heaven. [The ancient Greek poet] Hesiod thought of the heroes as half-way between gods and humans. Their mighty achievements inspired poets to suggest that human nature, far though it is from divinity, can yet come within reach of it.[1]

Through his exploits, therefore, the hero sets an example for normal people. He demonstrates that humans are potentially capable of doing great things if they will only set large goals and devote their whole energies to accomplishing them. Indeed, they have the potential of rising above their lowly natures and/or mundane surroundings, even if they cannot aspire to complete perfection or godhood.

As for the universality of the hero's adventure, Campbell broke it down into three essential parts —the separation, the initiation, and the return. "A hero ventures forth," he said,

> from the world of the common day into a region of supernatural wonder. Fabulous forces are there encountered and a decisive victory is won. The hero comes back from this mysterious adventure with the power to bestow boons on his fellow men.[2]

This threefold formula can be seen time and again in world mythology—in the Mesopotamian hero Gilgamesh's quest for the secret of immortality; in the victory of the Greek hero Theseus over the monstrous Minotaur, freeing his people from victimization by the creature; in the Celtic hero Cuchulainn's single-handed defense of his native kingdom against an army of invaders; and countless others. In all of these myths, the central character endures uncommon danger or hardship, attains a major goal, and

*Joseph Campbell, noted scholar of world mythology, observed that "The hero has a thousand faces."*

9

as a result human society benefits, either in the material sense or through the discovery of a great truth.

In fact, the hero always seeks to right a wrong or uncover the true nature of something. In this way, he brings freedom and justice for the oppressed, order out of chaos, or light from the darkness. Whether his face is Greek, Roman, Celtic, Chinese, Native American, or one of the thousand other guises he has been known to wear, he symbolizes human strivings for self-betterment and courage in the face of hardship. As mythologist Dorothy Norman puts it, the legends of heroes are "enlightened warnings to us to make the most of life, despite our limitations, and in the face of every catastrophe."[3]

# Mesopotamian Heroes: The Search for Immortality

Myths are probably as old as humanity, and for untold ages peoples in various regions of the world passed them from one generation to another by oral means. The first mythology ever written down was that of the Sumerians, who inhabited Mesopotamia (the "land between the rivers," the Tigris-Euphrates valley in what is now Iraq) some five thousand years ago. Recording this body of myths was possible because the Sumerians are credited with two of the greatest cultural advances in human history—the invention of writing and the development of literature. A hefty portion of that literature consisted of their myths, which were already very old when the art of writing itself was new.

The Sumerians' complex writing system appeared sometime between 3300 and 3000 B.C., perhaps in Uruk (northwest of the Persian Gulf), which many experts believe was the world's first true city. The invention then quickly spread to other parts of the Near East and eventually beyond. The initial process was simple but ingenious. Scribes used pointed sticks, styluses, or other objects to make impressions in moist clay tablets; and when the tablets dried and hardened, they became cumbersome but permanent records, the world's first versions of letters, account sheets, and books. In its most mature form, this writing system consisted mainly of small wedge-shaped marks arranged in various combinations. Modern scholars dubbed it "cuneiform" after the Latin word *cuneus*, meaning wedge- or nail-shaped.

Among the most important of the myths told in Sumerian cuneiform texts were those dealing with the larger-than-life exploits of the heroes Atrahasis, Gilgamesh, and Adapa.

# How Cuneiform Writing Was Deciphered

Here, from his *Civilization Before Greece and Rome*, historian and ancient languages expert H. W. F. Saggs briefly summarizes how modern scholars unraveled the mystery of cuneiform, the writing system the Sumerians and other Mesopotamian peoples used to record their myths.

*An example of cuneiform writing.*

*The decipherment of the wedge-shaped inscriptions set the learned world a challenge. There had been scholars working on it since the late eighteenth century. A Dane, Carsten Niebuhr, who traveled in Arabia and Persia in the 1770s, had noticed that at Persepolis in Persia [southern Iran] there were inscriptions on stone with three different forms of . . . [cuneiform] script. . . . Niebuhr observed that one of the forms . . . contained well under fifty different signs, and correctly deduced that it must be alphabetic. A young German scholar, G. F. Grotefend, worked on this script, and by 1802 . . . correctly [identified] about a third of the characters. The language was an early form of Persian. There was no significant advance upon Grotefend's partial decipherment until the 1840s, when a breakthrough was effected by . . . [English linguist] Henry Creswicke Rawlinson. . . . He spent his spare time copying inscriptions . . . in the three different scripts already mentioned . . . and in 1846 he was able to publish a paper giving a complete decipherment of the Old Persian alphabetic cuneiform. . . . But the two other scripts remained to be solved. Rawlinson recognized that one of these was obviously used for the language of Babylon, since the same system was found on the bricks from that city. We now call that language . . . Akkadian; Babylonian was one main dialect of it and Assyrian another. . . . In the long trilingual inscription, his decipherment of the Old Persian version gave him the general sense and a number of proper names. Using this and new inscriptions . . . Rawlinson had taken major steps toward the decipherment of Akkadian cuneiform by 1849. Other scholars were working on the script, and it quickly became possible to make out the sense of long texts and to begin to recover the details of the ancient history [and myths] of the two main kingdoms in the area in the first and second millennia B.C., Babylonia and Assyria.*

These, along with other Sumerian myths, became the common heritage of all later Mesopotamian cultures, including the Babylonians and Assyrians (who used cuneiform writing to record the language they shared—Akkadian). Some of the stories were eventually adopted by neighboring peoples, among them the Hebrews (who lived in Palestine, on the eastern Mediterranean coast), who incorporated them into their own literature (including the Old Testament). The most familiar of these to Western readers is the story of Atrahasis. He was the wise man and hero who saved humanity by building a large boat that enabled him and his family to survive a great flood sent by the gods. The Hebrews, of course, called him Noah.

The most important and influential of the Mesopotamian myths is the *Epic of Gilgamesh*. A large compilation of early heroic tales and folklore, it was first collected into a unified whole circa 2000 B.C. by an unknown Babylonian scribe. (Although written in Akkadian, rather than Sumerian, the themes, style, and names of the characters and places are Sumerian, showing that most of the content dates from Sumerian times.) The story centers on the exploits of the title character, Gilgamesh, who was probably originally a real Sumerian ruler, possibly the king of Uruk, as one legend states. In the epic, Gilgamesh performs several heroic feats, including his search for the secret of eternal life. The gift of immortality is also the theme of another heroic tale, that of Adapa, who attempts to win that gift for his people.

These and many other Mesopotamian myths deal with human attempts to understand and control the surrounding environment and to overcome personal limitations, such as the brevity of life. This fascination with immortality may stem from the fact that the region of Mesopotamia was prone to sudden disaster, and all the hard work of a

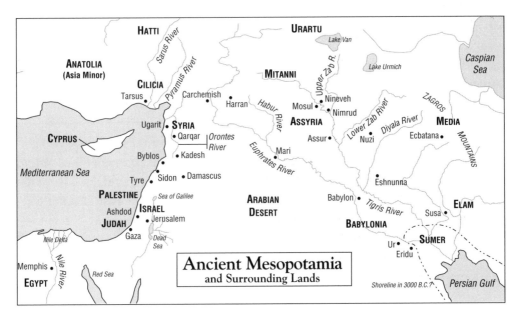

relatively short human lifetime might be erased in a frightening instant. According to noted Near Eastern scholar John Gray:

> Mesopotamia lay between the two capricious [unpredictable] river giants, Tigris and Euphrates, which could lay a district waste for a generation in one spring flood. It bordered the desert with its dust storms . . . locust swarms, and raiding Bedouin [nomadic desert tribesmen]. Thus the drama . . . of Mesopotamian mythology expresses the essentially emotional relationship of man to his environment in what we, though not he, would regard as both its natural and supernatural aspect.[4]

## Atrahasis and the Great Flood

The supernatural aspect of a destructive environment and the human attempt to resist and survive it are illustrated dramatically in the ancient story of Atrahasis. He was, like his father before him, the king of the Sumerian city of Shuruppak (in southern Mesopotamia). He did not begin life as a hero and savior but rose to the occasion when humanity was threatened by a catastrophe sent by the gods.

The trouble began when the powerful storm god Enlil (who was sometimes viewed as the leader or father of all the other gods) became alarmed at a vast increase in the human population. According to an account on a surviving cuneiform tablet:

> The country was as noisy as a bellowing bull [and] the God grew restless at their racket. Enlil had to listen to their noise. He addressed the great gods: "The noise of humanity has become too much. I am losing sleep over their racket. Give the order that disease shall break out."[5]

This move reduced the population as Enlil had hoped it would. But in time the humans multiplied once more, and the great god again became upset at their clamor, which was disturbing his quiet existence. He had the gods send drought and famine to plague humanity; but these catastrophes proved to be no more permanent than disease had been, for the human population, though significantly reduced in numbers, always ended up replenishing itself.

Finally Enlil decided that he must wipe out the humans completely with a great flood. Luckily for the proposed victims, however, Ea, god of wisdom and freshwater, sympathized with their plight and decided to help them behind Enlil's back. Ea approached Atrahasis and warned him of the coming deluge. The god instructed him to dismantle his house and use the material to construct a large boat. He should leave his everyday possessions behind and concentrate on trying to save living things in the ark. Ea advised the man to put aboard it the seeds of all the living things on the face of the earth.

The wise Atrahasis did as Ea had urged and built the ark. "I loaded her with everything there was," Atrahasis later recalled (in another surviving version of the story). "I

*An illustration portraying the Hebrew version of the great flood. In the story, the Mesopotamian god Ea urges Atrahasis to build an ark and put aboard it "the seeds of all living things."*

loaded her with all the seeds of living things, all of them. I put on board the boat all my kith and kin. I put on board the cattle from open country and all kinds of craftsmen."[6] No sooner had he completed this task when the destruction began. For six days and seven nights, the wind howled, torrents of rain flooded down on and covered the land, and millions of people and animals drowned.

Finally, on the seventh day, the storm subsided and Atrahasis sadly beheld the devastation wrought by the gods. "Silence reigned," he said,

for all of humanity had returned to clay. The flood-plain was as flat as a roof. I opened a porthole and light fell on my cheeks. I bent down, then sat. I wept. My tears ran down my cheeks. . . . The boat had come to rest on [the top of] Mount Nimush. . . . When the seventh day arrived, I put out and released a dove. The dove went; it came back, for no perching place was visible to it, and it turned around. [Later] I put out and released a raven. The raven went and saw the waters receding. And it ate . . . and did not turn round. Then I put all [on board the ark] out to the four winds [i.e., in all directions] and I made a sacrifice [to the gods].[7]

The gods' reactions to the salvation of humanity varied. Ishtar, goddess of love and war, was humbled by the event and swore by her colored necklace (i.e., the rainbow) that she would never forget it. Enlil, on the other hand, was at first angry that Ea had interfered in his plans to destroy the humans. The tactful Ea managed to calm the chief god, however. And to reward Atrahasis for his heroic deed, Enlil bestowed on that man and his wife (but no other humans) the gift of immortality.

## Gilgamesh Meets a Rival

Like Atrahasis, Gilgamesh did not start out as a hero. In fact, when Gilgamesh first became the king of the mighty city of Uruk,

## Was the Black Sea the Site of the Great Flood?

Most modern scholars agree that the great flood depicted in the myth of Atrahasis (the Hebrew Noah) was probably based on a real event. Around 5600–5500 B.C., Stone Age farmers from the mountainous regions bordering the northern rim of Mesopotamia began migrating southward into the Tigris and Euphrates plains, which were then largely uninhabited. The reasons for this migration are uncertain. But one provocative theory recently proposed by a group of scholars that includes Columbia University scientists William Ryan and Walter Pitman suggests they may have been escaping a natural catastrophe. The theory points to evidence showing that before the sixth millennium B.C., the Black Sea, located to the north of these mountains, was a large freshwater lake. Today that sea is joined to the Aegean and Mediterranean Seas via two straits, the Bosphorus and Dardanelles; but originally the Bosphorus was blocked by a huge earthen dam and the lake's level was hundreds of feet lower than that of the seas beyond. Geologic evidence shows that about 5600 B.C. the dam burst and mighty torrents of water rushed into the Black Sea lake, flooding its shores for many miles inland. Because the date of this catastrophic event roughly coincides with that of the initial migrations of peoples southward into Mesopotamia, Ryan and Pitman suggest that these population movements were set in motion by large numbers of refugees fleeing their lakeside villages and farms. They also speculate that over time the memory of the disaster gave rise to the Mesopotamian legends of the great flood. Though this scenario remains unproven, enough circumstantial evidence exists to warrant further serious research and discussion.

*Ruins of the ancient Sumerian city of Uruk. It was here that Gilgamesh became king and ruled his people with a heavy hand.*

he was not a popular ruler. Though he was a tremendously strong, skilled, and valiant warrior whom no other man dared to challenge to a fight, he had a weakness, namely, that no single woman could satisfy him. Showing no tact, sensitivity, or respect for the feelings of his people, he would snatch up young girls off the streets or from the fields and force them to have sex with him. This naturally raised the ire of the girls' families. But what could they do to remedy the situation? None dared to denounce the king for fear that he might punish or even kill them.

Finally, when they could stand Gilgamesh's outrages no longer, the city's elders went to the temple of the great mother goddess Aruru, who was Uruk's patron deity. There, they lay facedown before the goddess, who lounged serenely on her magnificent golden couch. The men beseeched her to create a rival for Gilgamesh, someone who could match his great strength and fighting skill. Let that rival challenge Gilgamesh, they suggested, and teach him a lesson so that the city could live in peace and security.

Aruru heard this plea and took pity on the beleaguered people of Uruk. As the elders watched in awe, she rose in all her shining majesty from her golden couch, strode outside, and exited the city gates. Eventually, having left the city and the sight of its residents far behind, she arrived at the riverbank. A surviving Babylonian account says that she

> washed her hands, pinched off a piece of clay, and cast it out into open country. [From the clay] she created a primitive man, Enkidu the warrior. . . . His whole body was shaggy with hair. . . . He knew

neither people nor country; he was dressed as cattle are [i.e., without clothes]. With gazelles, he eats vegetation, with cattle, he quenches his thirst at the watering place.[8]

It was not long before the people living in the villages on the outskirts of Uruk caught sight of this wild man roaming the nearby grasslands, and word soon reached the city. Gilgamesh himself heard about Enkidu and set for himself the goal of luring the stranger to Uruk and there civilizing him. The king accomplished the first part of the plan by sending a beautiful woman out into the wilderness. She found Enkidu, who, just as Gilgamesh had expected, fell for her good looks and considerable charms. She convinced the wild man to return with her to Uruk.

## The King Transformed

In the months that followed, Enkidu lived in Gilgamesh's palace in the city. The king's female servants and companions delighted in cutting the wild man's hair, dressing him in fine clothes, and teaching him table manners and other civilized customs. And indeed, fulfilling Gilgamesh's goal, Enkidu slowly but steadily became civilized.

However, the king had not counted on this unusual stranger becoming more civilized than Gilgamesh himself. This happened because the goddess Aruru had instilled in Enkidu a stronger sense of right and wrong than that possessed by the king. One night Gilgamesh invited Enkidu to go for a walk through the city with him and some other companions. When the king was about to enter a house without being invited (perhaps to force himself on another young woman), Enkidu barred his way. It would be best if Gilgamesh did not enter, Enkidu said. Instead, the two should just continue on their walk. But Gilgamesh was indignant and angry at being told what to do by one of his subjects. A terrible fight ensued, with the king and Enkidu wrestling each other in the street, crashing into walls, and breaking doorposts into showers of splinters. To the surprise of Gilgamesh and those watching the contest, Enkidu proved the king's equal in strength, fighting skill, and courage.

Eventually, the match ended in a draw. And the two men, having gained much mutual respect, became instant, inseparable friends. Moreover, Gilgamesh suddenly saw the evil and futility of his old ways and became a model ruler, causing his subjects to cheer and praise him whenever he appeared in public. Clearly, the goddess's plan had worked, for in the process of transforming Enkidu, Gilgamesh had himself been transformed.

It was clear to all, even to the gods, that these were not ordinary men, but heroes. At the request of Shamash, the sun god, Gilgamesh and Enkidu set out together on a heroic mission—to kill a monster named Huwawa. This huge, dreadful creature was terrorizing the land of the Cedar Mountain, which lay many miles to the west of Mesopotamia. The heroes made the journey, and in a titanic battle they slew the beast. This victory won them the heartfelt thanks of the people of that land, as well as the respect of Shamash, who had proposed the venture.

But another deity turned out to be much less friendly to Gilgamesh and Enkidu. Ishtar tried to take Gilgamesh as a lover; and when he refused, she decided to punish him by unleashing a giant bull on the city of Uruk. The two heroes managed to kill the bull. But this only further angered the goddess, who placed a deadly curse on Enkidu, causing him to fall ill and die. Gilgamesh was devastated and stricken with grief, and a long, mournful lament flowed from his lips. "For you, Enkidu," he said, tears rolling down his cheeks,

> I, like your mother . . . will weep. . . . Listen to me, elders of Uruk, listen to me! I myself must weep for Enkidu my friend, mourn bitterly like a wailing woman. . . . I touch his heart, but it does not beat at all. . . . I will lay you, Enkidu, on a bed of loving care. . . . Princes of the earth will kiss your feet. . . . I will fill the proud people with sorrow for you. And I myself will neglect my appearance after your death. Clad only in a lionskin, I will roam the open country.[9]

## A Hard Lesson Reveals an Essential Truth

Keeping his word, Gilgamesh went forth into the desert and wandered for many weeks, all the while contemplating the meaning of death. If the valiant and good Enkidu could die, he reasoned, then Gilgamesh too,

and all his loyal subjects, and all people everywhere must someday face death. Surely, he thought, there had to be some way to keep this terrible fate from coming to pass. Suddenly Gilgamesh realized what his greatest and most heroic mission must be—to search out the secret of immortality so that he might save humanity from the scourge of death.

The determined king of Uruk felt confident that he knew the best place to begin his quest. Like many other people, he had heard that the gods had given the secret of eternal life to the former king of Shuruppak—Utnapishtim, whom some called Atrahasis, the "wise one." The problem was that Utnapishtim lived far to the west on an island in the great sea, and no human knew the location of that island. This obstacle did not deter Gilgamesh, however. He made a

*The sun god, Shamash (right), sent Gilgamesh and Enkidu on a heroic mission.*

*Gilgamesh, shown here in a bas-relief from ancient Assur, undertook a dangerous journey to uncover the secret of immortality.*

long, difficult, and dangerous journey that consumed many months and forced him to confront an army of scorpion-men, to traverse a dark tunnel leading through the bowels of a huge mountain, and to journey through the "waters of death" that led to Utnapishtim's island.

Finally the brave and persistent Gilgamesh arrived at the island and confronted Utnapishtim. The old man seemed to know already why he had come and proceeded to tell him how he, Utnapishtim, had become the only immortal human being. He recounted the familiar story of how he had saved humanity by building an ark, in which he and his family and a few others had survived the great flood sent by the gods. Utnapishtim told the visitor that the gods had granted him eternal life as a special gift, so it was not possible for all people to acquire immortality. And even if they could, they would not enjoy it, for it was exceedingly difficult to find interesting things to do for eternity!

But Gilgamesh would not be put off. He managed to persuade the old man to reveal the existence and location of the "flower of youth," which would give eternal life to anyone who tasted it. The flower grew at the bottom of the sea, said Utnapishtim, at such a depth that no mortal person could hold his breath long enough to reach it. What the old man did not know was that Gilgamesh's strength and courage far exceeded that of ordinary mortals. Indeed, the king of Uruk wasted no time in diving into the sea and retrieving the magical flower.

After thanking Utnapishtim, Gilgamesh set out for home. Never once did he consider tasting the flower himself, for his only thought was to bestow this marvelous gift on all of his people. After the passage of many months, he had made it to within a few miles of Uruk when he decided to rest beside a small lake. Placing the flower on a rock, he dove into the water to refresh himself after his long, dusty journey. When he returned to the rock, however, he was just in time to see a snake swiftly slithering away, the flower clenched in its jaws. No matter how hard he tried, the man could not find the snake and had to enter his native city empty-handed. The greatest hero of the land had failed in his ultimate quest. Yet he had learned a valuable, if hard, lesson and in so doing revealed an essential truth to his people and all future generations: Only the gods are immortal; all human beings—no matter how powerful, or good, or brave—must face death in the end.

## Adapa's Fateful Visit to Heaven

Another prominent mortal, Adapa, learned this same hard lesson, although in a different way. Adapa was a wise man, a fisherman, and perhaps also a priest who lived in the city of Eridu (lying several miles southeast of Uruk). As an upstanding citizen and gods-fearing individual, one of his regular tasks was to keep Eridu's temple of Ea (god of freshwater) stocked with fresh food to use in sacrifices.

One day the man took his small boat out onto the blue-green waters of the Persian Gulf, hoping to catch some fish for the temple. At first the day was sunny and the waters calm, which was just the way Adapa liked it. But suddenly the deity known as the South Wind appeared and flapped its huge wings, causing a strong gale to blow over the gulf. Poor Adapa was unprepared and his boat capsized, sending him plunging into the cold water. Losing his temper, the normally wise man did something quite *unwise*, namely, he uttered a curse against

the South Wind, one so mean-spirited that it succeeded in breaking one of its wings. (In those days people believed that under the right conditions curses could cause harm to others.) The South Wind was injured so badly that for seven days it was unable to send its breezes blowing toward the land, an unusual situation that caught the attention of the great sky god, Anu. Angry that Adapa had dared to attack a divine personage, Anu ordered Ea to bring Adapa to his throne room in the sky and face punishment.

Ea and Adapa spoke at length about the situation. They both agreed that it was not every day that a human had the chance to ascend into heaven without dying first; so this appeared to be Adapa's big chance to become a hero to humanity by bringing back the secret of immortality, which Anu had the power to give him. The problem, of course, was that Anu was presently very upset with Adapa and in no mood to award him gifts. The man asked Ea what could be done to calm Anu and get on his good side. Ea told him not to fear, for he had a plan to do just that. According to a cuneiform tablet found in ancient Assyria, Ea gave the man the following instructions:

Wear your hair long and put on mourning garb. When you go up to heaven [and] when you approach the Gate of Anu, [the divine gate-keepers] Dumuzi and Gizzida [who used to live on earth] will be standing at the gate. They will see you and ask you questions, such as "On

21

whose behalf do you wear mourning garb?" [You must answer,] "Two gods have vanished from our country, and that is why I am in mourning." [They will ask,] "Who are the two gods who have vanished from your country?" [You must answer,] "They are Dumuzi and Gizzida." They [will be so flattered that they] will speak a word in your favor to Anu, and will present you to Anu in a good mood.[10]

This part of Ea's plan worked perfectly. Adapa approached the gate, spoke with Dumuzi and Gizzida, and they convinced Anu to forgive Adapa for injuring the South Wind. In fact, they argued, the man should be rewarded for his sincere love and respect for the gods. Anu's mood did indeed change, and he was prepared to reward Adapa; but here is where the second part of Ea's plan backfired. Ea had told the man that when he came before Anu, the great god would offer him refreshments. These would be the food and drink of death, Ea had warned, so the man should not accept them. So Adapa did just as Ea had said he should and refused Anu's hospitality.

Only later, after he had returned to Eridu, did the man learn, to his dismay and sadness, that Anu had not offered him the food and drink of death, but instead the food and drink of life, the secret of immor-

## Finding Gilgamesh's Missing Pieces

The greatest Mesopotamian mythological work, *The Epic of Gilgamesh*, was first translated in 1872 by English scholar and archaeologist George Smith. Of the work's approximately thirty-five hundred lines, about fifteen remained missing at the time Smith made his translation. Both scholars and the educated community considered the epic to be so important that a newspaper, the *Daily Telegraph*, financed an expedition to Iraq to find the missing lines. In an extraordinary turn of good fortune, the team, led by Smith himself, achieved its goal in the first few weeks of digging. In notes first published in 1875 (and later quoted in C. W. Ceram's *Hands on the Past*), Smith wrote:

*On the 14th of May . . . I sat down to examine the store of fragments of cuneiform inscriptions from the day's digging, taking out and brushing off the earth from the fragments to read their contents. On cleaning one of them I found to my surprise and gratification that it contained the greater portion of seventeen lines of inscription belonging to the first column of the Chaldean [Babylonian] account of the Deluge [great flood], and fitting into the only place where there was a serious blank in the story. When I had first published the account of this tablet I had conjectured that there were about fifteen lines wanting [lacking] in this part of the story, and now with this portion I was enabled to make it nearly complete.*

tality itself. Adapa's people, as well as future generations, could never be sure if Ea had purposely tricked the fisherman or had simply made a mistake. Two things were certain, however: The gods work in mysterious ways, and humans are not destined to enjoy eternal life. Like Atrahasis, Gilgamesh, and other true heroes, Adapa had learned these great truths the hard way, and his fellow humans benefited from his efforts.

# Greek Heroes: Valiant Warriors in a Golden Age

## Chapter Two

Almost everyone, young or old, in modern Western countries like the United States, Italy, France, and England is familiar with at least a few of the characters, images, or stories of ancient Greek mythology. This is partly because the Greeks laid much of the foundation for Western culture. And hundreds of surviving images from their folklore continue to pervade our literature, entertainment, and even commercial advertising. Among the more familiar are greedy King Midas, whose touch turned everything, even his food, into gold; Pegasus the flying horse, long recognized as the symbol for the Mobil Oil Company; the messenger god Hermes, whose winged cap and shoes allowed him to travel at breakneck speeds; and the heroic strongman Heracles, who, under his Roman name—Hercules—had his own long-running television show.

Heracles was only one of numerous heroes whose personalities and exploits constitute one of the two main categories of Greek mythology (the other being the gods and their own exploits). The Greek hero often interacted with gods who possessed human-like physical attributes, emotions, character flaws, and other traits. This was because the Greeks pictured their gods as being essentially like themselves, except for a tremendous difference in stature and power; the great power these divinities wielded could either provide for and maintain human civilization or utterly destroy it. The Greek hero fell somewhere between gods and humans, being stronger and more noble than an ordinary person, but less powerful than a god. (Heracles himself constituted an exception because he eventually *became* a god.)

Another unique characteristic of Greece's mythical heroes, and Greek mythology in general, was the way the classical Greeks viewed their origins. The term *classical* usually refers to the era in which ancient Greek city-states, most notably Athens, produced democratic ideals and great art, architecture, and literature—roughly the sixth through the fourth centuries B.C. This splendid society of Pericles, Socrates, Plato, and the imposing Parthenon temple looked back into the dim past at what it called the "Age of Heroes." This was a sort of golden age in which noble, exceedingly valiant warriors interacted with the gods and performed

mighty deeds. The later Greeks believed that this marvelous heroic world eventually passed away, giving way to their own age, which they saw as markedly inferior in all respects.

Modern scholars have shown that the bygone society of heroes idolized by the classical Greeks was in fact a distorted, exaggerated memory of a real society, one inhabited by humans just as ordinary as the later Greeks. A thousand years before Plato and his contemporaries were born, Greece and the Aegean island sphere had been the

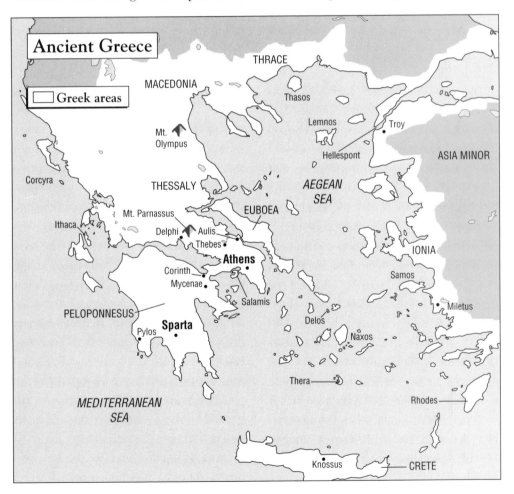

home of an impressive civilization. In the Bronze Age (when people used weapons and tools made of bronze), a culturally advanced people now called the Minoans built magnificent palaces on Crete and, with their huge fleets of cargo vessels and warships, dominated the region. For a long time they exerted a strong cultural influence on the Mycenaeans, who lived on the Greek mainland and spoke an early version of Greek. Vague memories of the interactions of these two cultures survived the centuries in the form of myths.

In fact, nearly all of the heroic characters and events of Greek mythology come from the Bronze Age. Among the most famous of these heroes was Theseus, supposedly an early king of Athens. In his most famous myth, told here, he rescues Athenian hostages held on the island of Crete, which may be based on an actual Mycenaean expedition against the Minoans. Among the main sources of his story are tracts by the first-century A.D. Greek biographer Plutarch and the second-century A.D. Greek writer Apollodorus. Also included here is the famous story of the labors of Heracles, as originally told by Apollodorus; and the equally famous fight to the finish between the heroes Achilles and Hector before the walls of Troy. The latter comes from the *Iliad*, a magnificent epic poem by the legendary bard Homer. The Trojan war he depicted, in which several Greek kings besieged the mighty city of Troy (in Asia Minor, what is now Turkey), may be based on an actual military expedition or raid conducted by Bronze Age Mycenaean warlords.

## Theseus Becomes a Hero

Long before the advent of the great war at Troy, there arose in Greece one of its finest and most valiant early champions—Athens's national hero, Theseus. To understand how he first became a hero, we must begin in the days shortly before his birth. His father, Aegeus, king of Athens, was traveling through southern Greece, heading for home after a long journey, and he stopped for the night at the house of a friend, Pittheus. That night Aegeus slept with Pittheus's daughter, Aethra, who then became pregnant. Before leaving for Athens, Aegeus placed one of his swords under a large stone and instructed Aethra that if the child was a boy, she should tell him about the sword. When he grew old and strong enough to lift the stone and retrieve the sword, the king said, she should send the boy to Athens to seek out his father.

Aegeus returned to Athens and many years passed. The child, who was indeed a boy, whom Aethra named Theseus, grew into a handsome, exceedingly intelligent, and admirable young man. When he felt he was ready, he easily lifted the stone and took possession of the sword, then eagerly set out for Athens. On the way, he decided that it would be best if he could prove himself a great hero before arriving, so that the father he had never met would be both impressed and proud of him. The young man had heard that several murderous bandits roamed the countryside on the road to Athens, terrorizing and killing travelers, farmers, and other innocent people. Setting himself the challenge of ridding the land of these brigands, one by one he met and defeated them.

According to Apollodorus, Theseus first overcame Periphetes,

> who, because of the club that he carried, was called the club-bearer. Since his legs were weak, Periphetes carried a club of iron and used it to kill passers-by. After he took the club away from him, Theseus continued to carry it himself. Second, Theseus killed Sinis . . . who was called the pine-bender . . . for he forced travelers to hold onto pine trees he had bent down. They, however, were not strong enough to do this and so they were pulled up to their deaths by the trees. Theseus killed Sinis in this same way.[11]

Theseus also defeated and slew several other unsavory characters. One was Sciron, who kicked passersby over the edge of a cliff; the young hero tossed him off the same cliff. Another offender, Cercyon, was a skilled wrestler who forced travelers to fight him and almost always ended up killing them. Theseus accepted this challenge and smashed his opponent against some rocks.

Because of these impressive deeds, Theseus's reputation preceded him; and when he reached Athens, the people of that city welcomed him with open arms. Of course, neither they nor their king, Aegeus, were yet aware of the young man's true identity. This was revealed at a banquet thrown by the king in honor of Theseus's heroic slaying of the bandits. In a dramatic gesture, the young

*Theseus (standing, left) saves some Athenian hostages held in Crete.*

man drew his sword; Aegeus instantly recognized it as the one he had placed under the stone, and the king joyfully announced that Theseus was his son and heir.

## The Labyrinth and the Minotaur

Once he had become settled in his new and rightful home city, Theseus learned to his dismay about a terrible injustice to which his people were regularly subjected. Several years before, Minos, the powerful king of the island kingdom of Crete, had visited Athens along with his own son, Androgeus. Unfortunately, Androgeus had suffered a fatal accident while on a bull hunt sponsored by Aegeus. Blaming the Athenian king and his city for this loss, Minos invaded Athens. He threatened to destroy the city if Aegeus did not agree to send seven young men and seven young women to Crete every nine years as tribute (payment acknowledging submission). Once they arrived in Crete, these hostages were locked in the Labyrinth, a mazelike dungeon inhabited by a fierce creature—the Minotaur, which was half man and half bull. One by one, the Minotaur would hunt down and devour the captives. By the time that Theseus arrived in Athens, this grisly scenario had played out twice.

Theseus decided that he must free his city from this appalling obligation. When the time came for the third group of hostages to make their way to certain death in Crete, Theseus volunteered to become one of their number, promising to do everything in his power to slay the Minotaur. Old Aegeus was

grateful, but he worried about what might happen to his son. "On the two earlier occasions," Plutarch wrote,

> there had seemed to be no hope of deliverance [for the hostages], and so the Athenians had sent out their ship with a black sail, believing that it was carrying their youth to certain doom. But this time Theseus urged his father to take heart and boasted that he would overcome the Minotaur, and so Aegeus gave the [ship's] pilot a second sail, a white one, and ordered him on the return voyage to hoist the white canvas if Theseus were safe, but otherwise to sail with the black [canvas] as a sign of mourning.[12]

Bidding farewell to his father, Theseus sailed with the other hostages for Crete. There, before putting them into the Labyrinth, the authorities paraded the doomed young men and women before the local populace. Among those watching was King Minos's daughter, the princess Ariadne, who fell in love with Theseus at first sight and became determined to save him somehow from the fate ordained by her father. That night she went to the young man and told him of her love. She also brought along a means by which he could find his way out of the Labyrinth—a ball of twine, which, she said, he should tie to the door and unravel as he walked along; later he would be able to retrace his steps by following the trail of twine.

*This Roman floor mosaic from the first century* A.D. *shows Theseus slaying the Minotaur.*

Unraveling the ball of twine as Ariadne had instructed, Theseus descended into the Labyrinth the next morning and sought out the Minotaur. Finding the repulsive creature, he engaged it in hand-to-hand combat and succeeded in beating it to death with his fists (since he lacked a sword or other weapon). Wasting no time, Theseus led the Athenian hostages out of the Labyrinth by following the twine. Reaching the light of day, they joined Ariadne, who was waiting for them, boarded the Athenian ship, and escaped.

On the way to Athens, the party stopped at the island of Naxos to rest. There, they unfortunately lost Ariadne. The way this happened varies from one ancient source to another, one saying that Theseus abandoned her, another that he got lost in a storm and returned to find her dead, and still another that the fertility god Dionysus fell in love with her and carried her away.

All the versions agree, however, on what happened when the ship made it back to Athens. "In his distress over losing Ariadne," Apollodorus claims,

> Theseus forgot as he was sailing back to port to hoist the white sail on his ship. Aegeus, therefore, when he caught sight of the ship from the top of the Acropolis [Athens's central,

rocky hill] and saw the black sail, thought Theseus had been killed, and so he jumped to his death.[13]

To commemorate the tragic demise of poor old Aegeus, the body of water bordering Athenian territory became known as the Aegean Sea, the name it has borne ever since.

## The Madness of Heracles

In the days when the hero Theseus ruled Athens after his father's death, there lived the strongest man in Greece—Heracles, whom many Greeks, both at the time and in later ages, viewed as the greatest hero of all.

## Differing Versions of Ariadne's Fate

Here, from his biography of Theseus (Ian Scott-Kilvert's translation in *The Rise and Fall of Athens*), Plutarch lists the various and conflicting versions of Ariadne's fate that were current in his own time (the first century A.D.).

*There are many different accounts of . . . the story of Ariadne, none of which agree in their details. According to some versions she hanged herself when Theseus deserted her, while others tell us that she was taken to Naxos by sailors, that she lived there with Oenarus, the priest of [the fertility god] Dionysus, and that Theseus had abandoned her because he was in love with another woman. . . . There are others who say that Ariadne actually bore two sons to Theseus, Oenopion and Staphylus. . . . [Still another version] says that Theseus was driven off his course by a storm to [the island of] Cyprus, that Ariadne, who was pregnant and was suffering terribly from the motions of the ship, was put on shore by herself, and that Theseus, while trying to rescue the vessel, was swept out to sea again. . . . She died before the child was born, they [the Naxians] buried her . . . [and] Theseus returned later and was overcome with grief. . . . Some of the Naxian writers also have a version of their own, to the effect that there were really two . . . Ariadnes. One of these, they say, was married to Dionysus in Naxos . . . while the other at a later date was carried off by Theseus and deserted by him.*

Not only were his physical strength and prowess unmatched, but he was a humble man who owned up to his mistakes and willingly endured all manner of punishments, usually self-inflicted, as penance. Still, he was not a completely perfect hero. This was because he possessed two character flaws, the first being a lack of keen intelligence like that of Theseus. As the famous modern mythologist Edith Hamilton puts it, Heracles

> could never have thought out any new or great idea as the Athenian hero was held to have done. Heracles' thinking was limited to devising a way to kill a monster which was threatening to kill him. Nevertheless, he had true greatness. Not because he had complete courage based on overwhelming strength, which is a matter of course, but because, by his sorrow for wrongdoing and his willingness to do anything to expiate [atone for] it, he showed greatness of soul. If only he had had some greatness of mind as well . . . he would have been the perfect hero.[14]

Heracles' other flaw was his temper. On occasion he flew into uncontrollable rages during which he struck out at and hurt whoever was near him, even family, friends, and innocent bystanders. This is what caused the tragedy that inspired his most famous exploits—the twelve labors.

The series of events leading to these labors began when Heracles helped the people of

*The head of Hercules, as depicted by the famous Greek sculptor Glykon.*

the city of Thebes (northwest of Athens), who rewarded him by giving him the hand of their princess, Megara, in marriage. Heracles came to love her deeply, and she bore him three fine sons, whom he cared for just as much. Unfortunately, the strongman had an archenemy—Hera, wife of Zeus, the leader of the gods. She hated Heracles because he had been born of the union of Zeus and a mortal woman (one of that god's many mistresses), and she often went out of her way to cause the hero grief. Seeing his deep feelings for his family, the jealous goddess caused him to fall into a temper tantrum worse than any he had experienced before. And in this fit of temporary insanity, Heracles killed his wife and sons with his bare hands.

*The ruins of ancient Mycenae. The Oracle of Delphi told Heracles to seek out Eurystheus, the king of Mycenae.*

When he finally came to his senses and saw his mangled family members lying at his feet, Heracles was beside himself with guilt and anguish. In his tortured mind, killing himself seemed the only just punishment for so terrible a crime. But just as he was about to do away with himself, his friend, the Athenian hero Theseus, arrived and took his bloody hands in his own. Theseus implored the strongman not to go through with it and take his own life. Heracles responded that he had committed a horrible crime and should suffer death himself so that their deaths might be properly avenged. But Theseus argued that what Heracles had done was not murder, since he had been bewitched and therefore did

not realize what he was doing. He urged the strongman to go with him to Athens, where a champion of his caliber was badly needed.

## The Delphic Oracle Dispenses Advice

Heracles reluctantly agreed to go to Athens with Theseus. But though the people of that great city welcomed the strongman and told him that the deaths of his wife and sons were not his fault, he could not bring himself to agree with them. In his own mind, he remained a criminal who must be punished. Seeking advice on what he might do to atone for the killings, he left Athens and journeyed westward to Delphi, where the temple of Apollo, god of prophecy and healing, was located. In that temple dwelled the famous oracle, a priestess who acted as a medium between the god and humans. She told Heracles to go to Mycenae, in southern Greece, and seek out its king, Eurystheus. He would devise a series of extremely difficult tasks, and only after Heracles had completed them would he be cleansed of the guilt of his terrible crime.

Following the oracle's advice, Heracles made his way to the fortress-town of Mycenae, whose mammoth stone walls perched atop a rocky crag overlooking a fertile valley in southeastern Greece. Eurystheus welcomed the strongman and told him that he must perform a number of labors that an ordinary person would find daunting or even impossible. The first was to kill the Nemean Lion, a huge creature that could not be wounded by weapons. Heracles walked to Nemea (which lay a few miles northwest of Mycenae), and there found the huge and fearsome creature guarding its lair in a cave on the side of a mountain. At first the strongman tried shooting it with his bow, but sure enough, the arrows from the weapon had no effect. Since weapons would not work, Heracles decided to fight without them. He charged forward, grasped the lion around its neck, and strangled it.

When Heracles returned to Mycenae carrying the carcass of the Nemean Lion on his back, the people were astounded. Eurystheus praised him for a job well done but was careful to point out that his labors had only just begun. According to Apollodorus:

For his second labor, Eurystheus ordered Heracles to kill the Hydra of Lerna [located several miles southwest of Mycenae], which lived in the swamp of Lerna and went out into the countryside killing cattle and laying waste to the land. The Hydra had an enormous body and nine heads, one of which was immortal. Heracles went to Lerna . . . and found the Hydra on the brow of a hill . . . where it had its den. Shooting at it with flaming arrows, Heracles drove the creature out, and then, when it came close, he grabbed it and held it tight. But the

*In his second labor, Heracles slew the Hydra of Lerna.*

Hydra wrapped itself around his foot, and he was not able to get free by striking off its heads with his club, for as soon as one head was cut off two grew in its place. In addition, a huge crab came to the aid of the Hydra and kept biting Heracles' foot. He therefore killed the crab and . . . set fire to the woods nearby and, by burning the stumps of the Hydra's heads with firebrands, kept them from growing out again. Then Heracles cut off the immortal head, and when he had buried it in the ground, he put a heavy rock over it. Then he split open the body of the Hydra and dipped his arrows in its poison.[15]

## The Gift of Eternal Life

Heracles returned in triumph to Mycenae once more. Was there a third labor to perform? he asked Eurystheus. Indeed there was—to bring back alive a fabulous stag with horns of gold, a creature sacred to the goddess of the hunt, Artemis. Although the strong-

man managed to complete this difficult task, it took him an entire year. The king of Mycenae then proceeded to heap still more labors on Heracles, who patiently and humbly accepted them all without complaint, for this was the penance he had agreed on.

For his fourth labor, Heracles tracked down and captured a large and vicious boar that was destroying the villages and the farmlands near Mount Erymanthos, in a desolate region many miles to the west of Mycenae. For his fifth task, he cleaned the stables of Augeas, king of Elis (a city lying west of Mount Erymanthos), which were unbelievably filthy after thousands of cattle had lived in them for years. To accomplish this task, Apollodorus says, he "tore away part of the foundations of the stable and diverted the Alpheus and Peneus rivers into the stables, letting them run out through an opening he had made on the other side."[16] Then Heracles drove away a flock of huge birds that were plaguing the people of Stymphalus (northwest of Nemea) to fulfill his sixth labor. And to complete his seventh task, he journeyed to Crete and captured a beautiful but savage bull that the sea god,

*This first century B.C. sarcophagus in Rome shows Heracles performing five of his twelve labors.*

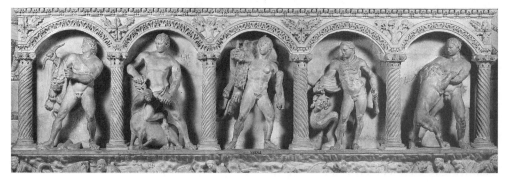

*In his seventh labor for Eurystheus, Heracles captured a savage cretan bull and brought it back to Mycenae.*

Poseidon, had given to that island's king, Minos. The eighth labor that Eurystheus ordered the strongman to perform was to go to Thrace, in extreme northern Greece, and bring back a herd of man-eating horses belonging to Diomedes, the king of a pow-erful Thracian tribe. With great difficulty but unerring determination, Heracles slew Diomedes and captured the horses.

Even after Heracles had delivered these bloodthirsty creatures to Eurystheus in Mycenae, his punishment was not over. In fact, he had to endure four more labors, for a total of twelve. These last four, like the seventh and eighth, required him to bring back various creatures or objects to Mycenae. In the ninth labor, Heracles delivered to Eurystheus the girdle of Hippolyta, queen of the Amazons, a tribe of warrior women who inhabited the wild steppes of the region north of Thrace. The tenth labor required the hero to travel all the way to the western end of the Mediterranean Sea. There, he captured the cattle of a monster named Geryon (who had three bodies and three heads). And on his way back, Heracles commemorated the deed by setting up two gigantic rocks at the sea's mouth, which became known as the Pillars of Heracles (today called Gibraltar). The eleventh labor brought into the strongman's grasp a treasure trove of golden apples; and the twelfth witnessed his descent into the dark and forbidding underworld to capture Cerberus, the monstrous and vicious three-headed dog that guarded that realm of death. (After bringing Cerberus to Mycenae, Heracles had to take it back to the underworld, since Eurystheus had no intention of keeping the dangerous creature.)

Heracles completed all twelve of these seemingly impossible labors, a task that had consumed many years and took him to the ends of the earth. During all that time he never wavered because he still felt strongly that he must atone for killing his wife and sons. Now that he had in fact atoned, however, his adventures were far from over; for in the years that followed, he performed numerous other formidable and wondrous deeds. Finally, after he had been badly burned by the caustic blood of a centaur (a creature that was half man and half horse), the great hero decided that he had had enough of mortal life. He asked his friends to erect a large funeral pyre and care-

*In this nineteenth century engraving, Heracles lies down on his funeral pyre.*

fully laid down on it. Then he gave his bow and arrows to a faithful young follower, Philoctetes, who set the pyre ablaze. A few moments later, the sad mourners were startled by a huge bolt of lightning that exploded above the pyre, after which they witnessed a column of smoke rise swiftly into the sky. When they looked back at the pyre, the body of their friend was nowhere to be seen, and they suddenly realized, with great joy, what had happened. The gods had taken the mighty and big-hearted Heracles into their bosom, granting him the gift of eternal life.

## Hector Slays Patroclus

Heracles was not the only great hero of those times, however. Many warriors and heroes came together in this age for the purpose of fighting the Trojan War, which had begun after the Trojan prince Paris had abducted the Greek queen Helen. Among these heroes, none were greater than the Greek warrior Achilles and the Trojan prince Hector (Paris's brother), who eventually faced each other in a fight to the death. The immediate series of events that led to this dramatic and crucial confrontation was as follows. After the Greeks had besieged Troy for over nine years, resulting in a virtual stalemate, Achilles had a loud and bitter quarrel with Agamemnon, king of Mycenae and the supreme commander of the Greek forces. In a huff, Achilles retired to his tent and refused to come out and lead the Greek forces in battle as he had so often done. This put the Greeks at a serious disadvantage, for Achilles was their greatest warrior, and his absence hurt morale.

While Achilles was indisposed, Agamemnon unwisely decided to lead an attack on the Trojans on his own, and a large-scale battle took place before the city's towering walls. During this fighting, mighty Hector, son of Priam, king of Troy, entered the fray and led the Trojans in an irresistible offensive that drove the Greeks off the field and back nearly to their beach encampment. Pressed hard by the Trojan forces, the Greeks were now in a perilous position, and in despair Agamemnon proposed that his own army give up the fight and return to Greece. The events of the following day only seemed to confirm that this would be the best course. The Trojans crashed through the stockade protecting the Greek camp and forced many of the Greeks to retreat to their ships. Hector was wounded by the powerful Greek warrior Ajax, but the healing god Apollo soon revived the Trojan champion, making him stronger than ever. "All afire, blazing from head to foot" is how Homer described Hector at that moment. He charged at the enemy "as a wave bursts down on a veering ship . . . showers of foam overwhelm the hull . . . the sailors quake, their hearts race on with terror." Indeed, the Greeks reacted with terror as Hector lunged at them, "like a murderous lion mad for kills, charging at helpless cattle."[17] Triumphantly, he led his men to the Greek ships and shouted, "Bring fire! Up with the war cries all together! Now Zeus hands us a day worth all the rest, for today we will seize these ships!"[18]

At this fateful juncture, with the Greek cause seemingly lost, another brave Greek warrior, Patroclus, approached his close friend Achilles, who was still brooding in his tent and refusing to fight. If Achilles would not enter the fray, said Patroclus, "at least send *me* into battle, quickly. Let the whole Myrmidon army [Achilles' own handpicked and much-feared warriors] follow my command." Then Patroclus pleaded, "Also give me your own fine armor to buckle on my back, so the Trojans might take *me* for you . . . and back off from their attack."[19]

Achilles agreed to Patroclus's request, and Patroclus, wearing his friend's armor, led the Myrmidons and other Greeks against the Trojans. Thinking that mighty Achilles himself was attacking them, the fearful Trojans began to fall back, just as Patroclus had predicted they would; even Hector could not withstand the force of the seemingly rejuvenated Greek army. But eventually the overconfident Patroclus found himself face-to-face with Hector himself, who was much the superior warrior. Hector easily slew Patroclus and stripped off Achilles' armor. Then after a desperate struggle for the body, the Greeks bore Patroclus back to their ships.

## Achilles and Hector Meet Face-to-Face

Hearing of his friend's death, the grief-stricken Achilles became a changed man. His mother, the sea goddess Thetis, rushed to Hephaestos, god of the forge, who swiftly created a new suit of armor for Achilles, this one even stronger and more beautifully ornamented than the one Patroclus had borrowed. Then Achilles went to Agamemnon, patched up their feud, and led his Myrmidons and the other Greeks in a mighty charge against the Trojan ranks. Many of the gods, backing one side or the other, joined in the fray. The Trojans, finally unable to withstand the Greek onslaught, fled back into the city; that is, with the exception of Hector, who stood alone outside the gates, waiting to face Achilles.

Hector did not have to wait long, for moments later Achilles rushed at him. The greatest Greek warrior looked so magnificent and fearsome in his armor that he resembled "the god of war . . . as the bronze around his body flared like a raging fire or the rising, blazing sun."[20] Seeing this formidable and frightening apparition bearing down on him, Hector momentarily lost his nerve. He turned and ran, and as thousands from both sides looked on, Achilles chased him round and round the city's walls.

Finally Hector stopped running and faced his pursuer. "No more running from you in fear, Achilles!" he declared. "Three times I fled around the great city of Priam. . . . Now my spirit stirs me to meet you face-to-face. Now kill or be killed!" Achilles answered him, saying, "Come, call up whatever courage you can muster. Life or death—now prove yourself a spearman, a daring man of war! . . . Now you'll pay at a stroke for all my comrades' grief, all of those warriors you killed in the fury of your spear!"[21]

With a thunderous crash of bronze on bronze, the two heroes came together in mortal combat. Cheers went up from the watching Greeks and Trojans, each side urging on its champion. Achilles was first to hurl his spear, but missed; then, in a mighty heave, Hector let loose his own spear, which hit his opponent's shield dead center but glanced off. Cursing, Hector drew his sword and, in Homer's words, "swooped like a soaring eagle launching down from the dark clouds to earth to snatch some helpless lamb."[22] Achilles charged too and searched for an opening somewhere on Hector's splendid body where he might thrust his spear, which he had managed to recover. Finally Hector's throat was momentarily exposed, and "there, as Hector charged in fury, brilliant Achilles drove his spear and the point went stabbing clean through the tender neck."[23] The greatest Trojan warrior now lay dead in the dust before his horrified countrymen's eyes. Completing his vengeance, Achilles stripped off his opponent's armor, tied the corpse to the back of his chariot, and triumphantly dragged it around the city walls.

In time, however, as Achilles' anger and blood-lust subsided, he agreed to give Hector's body to the grieving King Priam. The Trojans then conducted a solemn funeral for Hector, while at the same time the Greeks held final rites for brave Patroclus. The war continued, however; and eventually Achilles, like Hector, met his end in combat, as Prince Paris, who was an expert bowman, killed him with a

# The Struggle for Patroclus's Body

This excerpt from Book 17 of the *Iliad* (E. V. Rieu's translation) describes the fierce battle between the Greeks and Trojans for the body of the fallen hero Patroclus.

*Menelaus [king of Sparta] and [the young archer] Meriones labored to retrieve Patroclus's body from the [battle]field and bring it to the hollow ships, with the battle raging round them, fierce as a fire that in a moment blazes up, falls on a town and consumes the houses in a mighty conflagration. As the roaring wind beats on the flames, so did the ceaseless din from fighting men and horses beat upon them as they went. They struggled along with their burden like mules who put out all their strength to drag a log or some huge timber for a ship down from the mountains by a rocky track, tugging away till they nearly break their hearts, what with the labor and the sweat. Behind them the two Ajaxes [Ajax of Salamis and Ajax of Locris] held the enemy, as a wooded ridge that stretches out across the countryside holds back the floods. . . . Thus all the time the two Ajaxes fended off the Trojans who attacked the rear. But they were hard beset, and by two men in particular, [the gallant Trojan prince] Aeneas . . . and the illustrious Hector. . . . The Greek warriors with cries of terror fled before Aeneas and Hector, losing all stomach for the fight; and many a fine weapon was dropped . . . by the fleeing Greeks, who were given no respite from attack.*

# The Modern Rediscovery of Troy

While the ancient Greeks accepted that the Trojan War had been a real event, modern scholars of the eighteenth and nineteenth centuries believed that it and most of its characters were entirely mythical. Here, from his book *The Legend of Odysseus*, classical historian Peter Connolly tells how the real Troy came to light at a site called Hisarlik, in northwestern Turkey.

*Troy was discovered by an amateur archaeologist, Heinrich Schliemann, in 1870. He found several towns each built on the ruins of the previous one. At the second level up he discovered signs of burning and concluded that this was Homer's Troy. In 1882 Schliemann was joined by a professional archaeologist, Wilhelm Dörpfeld, and the excavating was soon left to him. Dörpfeld identified nine successive towns on the site and was able to show that Homer's Troy was between the sixth and seventh levels. Dörpfeld's findings were checked by an American expedition between 1932 and 1938. They agreed with his findings but improved techniques enabled them to identify no less than 30 different levels of occupation. . . . Experts disagree over which Troy was destroyed by the Mycenaeans. Was it [the level that scholars call] Troy VIh, a powerful and wealthy town with spacious, well-constructed buildings? This fits Homer's description but it appears to have been destroyed by an earthquake. Or was it Troy VIIa, the new town that rose out of the rubble? VIIa was poor and overpopulated. It was destroyed by fire after a life of only about thirty years. Its crudely built houses were huddled against the town walls. . . . These features indicate a siege mentality, with the people from the countryside crowding into the town for protection.*

*Heinrich Schliemann uncovered the ruins of Troy.*

well-aimed arrow. And in his turn, Paris met a similar fate when the Greek warrior Philoctetes, using the hugely powerful bow given to him by the legendary strongman Heracles shortly before his ascent into heaven, felled and killed the Trojan prince.

Ultimately, Achilles' defeat of Hector foreshadowed the outcome of the war itself, for later that year Troy finally fell to the victorious Greeks and thereafter entered the realm of legend. Both Achilles and Hector, like Theseus and Heracles before them, became legendary heroes in large part because they had displayed a level of courage and fighting skill far above that of ordinary men.

# Roman Heroes: Founders of the Eternal City

## Chapter Three

L ike all peoples in all ages, the ancient Romans wanted to believe that they were descended from characters of heroic stature. And their mythology, like that of the Greeks, was crowded with heroes who had performed valiant deeds in bygone eras. The major Roman myth-tellers had two main sources of inspiration, which resulted in the development of two broad thematic categories of Roman myths. The first of these sources was Greek mythology. When Rome's increasingly powerful empire absorbed the Greek states of the eastern Mediterranean in the last two centuries B.C., the Romans, who greatly admired Greek culture, eagerly absorbed many of the popular Greek myths. Making the transition an easy one was the fact that by that time a number of the Greek gods had been given Roman names and incorporated into Roman theology. For example, the Roman Jupiter, origi-

nally an Italian sky god, had come to be associated with the Greek Zeus, supreme leader of the gods; and the Roman Minerva had become the equivalent of Athena, Greek goddess of war. (The merging of Greek and Roman myths is referred to as "classical" mythology, just as Greco-Roman history and culture in general is called classical civilization.)

The other major inspiration for Roman mythology was early Roman history. Latin writers of Rome's golden age of literature, in the late first century B.C.—particularly Virgil in his epic poem the *Aeneid* and Livy in his famous history of Rome—glorified the city's founding fathers and their deeds in an epic manner. These stories, unlike most Greek myths, rarely depicted the gods getting involved in human endeavors; instead, they often immortalized local military and political heroes and members of illustrious

Roman families, in the process commenting on and attempting to perpetuate traditional moral values, such as simplicity, frugality, and patriotism. Whereas the Greek heroes had lived in the so-called "Age of Heroes," a remote era seen as superior to later ages, the deeds of the Roman heroes were seen as part of a mighty drama that was still unfolding in Virgil's day. Though Rome's past had been glorious, the Roman writers proclaimed, its present and future were even more noble and admirable. Thus, Roman writers managed to press a stamp of Roman individuality on classical mythology at the same time that they embellished and passed on the traditional Greek myths that had captured their imaginations.

Among the most important of the early Roman heroes was the founder and namesake of Rome, the so-called "eternal" city—Romulus. Livy told his story in his Roman history, as did the Greek biographer Plutarch (who flourished about a century after Livy). Two other noteworthy Roman champions were Horatius Cocles, who supposedly single-handedly saved Rome from an invading army; and Lucius Quinctius Cincinnatus, the great model of Roman agrarian simplicity and virtue (both of whose tales Livy told).

The greatest Roman hero of all—Aeneas—was not actually a Roman, however, but a Trojan. Though Romulus, Horatius, and other legendary Romans were impressive characters, the early Romans were well aware

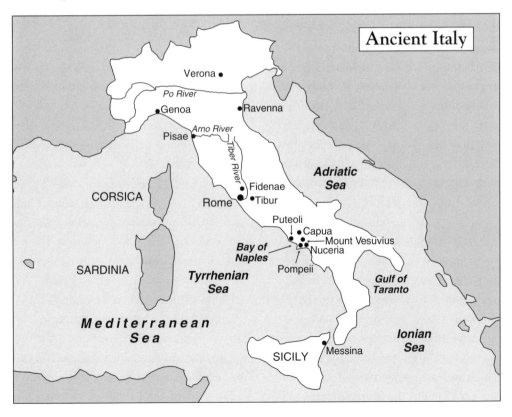

that these heroes did not quite compare in stature with some Greek ones. Several of the greatest Greek heroes had fought in the famous Trojan War. This momentous event from the Age of Heroes, in which a group of early Greek kings besieged the city of Troy (on the northwestern coast of what is now Turkey), was later immortalized by the Greek poet Homer in his epic poem the *Iliad*. Some of those who fought at Troy, such as the Greeks Achilles and Odysseus and the Trojans Hector and Aeneas, were viewed as men of enormous stature and valor, who had possessed the added distinction of having interacted directly with the gods.

To raise the stature of their own history, the Romans attempted to create a link between themselves and the Trojan War. At least by the sixth century B.C., it appears, Roman legends had incorporated the tale of the Trojan prince Aeneas's escape from the burning Troy and his fateful journey to Italy, where he became the founder of the Roman race. The longest and most magnificent telling of his story is Virgil's *Aeneid*. As for how this blatant adoption of a Greek tradition squared with Roman pride, the noted classical scholar T. J. Cornell comments:

> In general it is not surprising that the Romans were willing to embrace a story that flattered their pride by associating them with the legendary traditions of the Greeks, whose cultural superiority they were forced to acknowledge—albeit sometimes grudgingly. More specifically, in Greek myth Aeneas possessed qual-

*An ancient Roman mosaic depicting Virgil, the author of the* Aeneid.

ities which the Romans liked to see in themselves, such as reverence for the gods and love of his fatherland. The Trojan legend was also useful to the Romans in that it gave them a respectable identity in the eyes of a wider world, and one that could be used to advantage in their dealings with the Greeks. . . . Finally, we should note that by claiming to be Trojans the Romans were saying that they were not Greeks, and in a sense defining themselves in opposition to the Greeks. . . . In the hands of Virgil and other writers of the first century B.C. it became a means to reconcile them, and make Roman rule acceptable in the Greek world.[24]

## Aeneas Searches for a New Home

In Virgil's famous epic, Aeneas's fateful story begins seven years after the fall of Troy. The Trojan prince's small fleet of ships was plying the calm waters near the large island of Sicily, when the goddess Juno (wife of Jupiter) intervened. With her divine powers, she could foresee the awful possibility that Aeneas's descendants might destroy her favorite city, the lovely and prosperous North African metropolis of Carthage (a turn of events that actually occurred many centuries later). So she mustered up a violent storm, hoping to scatter and destroy Aeneas's vessels. As Virgil told it:

Darkness descended on the deep, thunder shackled the poles, the air crackled with fire, everywhere death was at the sailor's elbow. . . . The waves towered to the stars; the oars were smashed, the bow yawed . . . and a huge mountain of toppling water battered the vessels' beams.[25]

When the tempest finally subsided, Aeneas and his surviving followers made their way to the nearest shore, which, as fate would have it, turned out to be the coast near Carthage. The men entered the city and soon Aeneas met its queen, Dido, who fell madly in love with him. "His noble

*As the Greeks sack Troy Aeneas carries his father, Anchises, out of the burning city.*

blood and state," Virgil wrote, "his face and his voice were branded upon her breast, forbidding sleep."[26] At her request, Aeneas proceeded to tell her about how he had escaped the burning Troy carrying his aged father, Anchises, on his back. Having lost their home, he said, they had no other choice but to search for another, so they and their companions had built some ships.

Sailing out into the Aegean Sea, Aeneas recalled, the Trojan refugees made one of their initial stops at the tiny sacred island of Delos (which lies at the center of the Aegean). There, an oracle (a priestess who conveyed the words of the gods to humans) gave him a message from Apollo, god of prophecy and healing. The Trojans should seek out their "ancient mother," the message said, the land from which their distant ancestors had originally come. Thinking that this ancient motherland might be the island of Crete (which lies southeast of the Greek mainland), Aeneas led his followers there. But after they had landed, they received another message from Apollo, this one informing them:

> Since Troy was consumed [by fire], we [i.e., the gods] have followed you and your arms . . . and we shall raise your prosperity to the stars and give to your city its mighty sway. . . . There is a place the Greeks have called Hesperia—the western land—an ancient country powerful in war and rich of soil. . . . [The inhabitants call] themselves "Italians" after Italus—one of their leaders. There lies your true home.[27]

In this way, Aeneas learned that his fate was to sail to Italy and there to establish a new home for his people.

## Dido's Curse

Sailing westward, the Trojans stopped on one of a group of islands known as the Strophades. No sooner had they slaughtered some cattle, cooked the meat, and settled down for a meal, when a flock of Harpies appeared seemingly out of nowhere. These hideous, smelly, birdlike creatures, which had large sharp claws and women's faces, descended on the gathering and fouled the food by covering it with their sickening stench. Aeneas and his followers managed to drive the creatures away. But the retreating Harpies uttered a combination of prophecy and curse, saying that Aeneas would make it to Italy but would not be allowed to establish a walled city of his own until hunger had driven him to devour his tables. (When Aeneas and his followers later sailed up the Tiber River in Italy, they stopped to eat and were so hungry that after finishing their meal, they ate the thin breadcakes they were using as platters; Aeneas interpreted these as their "tables" and concluded that the Harpies' prophecy had been fulfilled.)

After the Harpies had departed, Aeneas continued westward, constantly harassed by the goddess Juno, who still harbored resentment toward Aeneas and the other Trojans. Eventually, Aeneas said, finishing the story of his recent adventures, the travelers reached Carthage and met Queen Dido. Delighted with the tale and now even more in love with

# Jupiter, Greatest of Gods and Friend to Rome

According to legend, as told in Virgil's Aeneid, the god Jupiter ordains that Aeneas will journey to Italy and there establish the noble Roman race. That the Romans claimed to enjoy Jupiter's favor is not surprising, for that god was the supreme deity of the Roman state pantheon (group of gods). Originally an Italian sky god thought to cause rain and lightning and to oversee agriculture, over the years Jupiter became increasingly powerful and important in Roman eyes. During the Roman Monarchy (which ended in 509 B.C. with the establishment of the Roman Republic), there developed the cult of Jupiter Optimus Maximus (the "best and greatest" of all Jupiters), part of the Capitoline Triad. The Triad, or group of three, included two other prominent deities—Juno, Jupiter's wife, and Minerva, goddess of handicrafts and war. (The principal temple to Jupiter and the Triad was located on Rome's Capitoline Hill, where generals deposited the spoils of war and the Senate held its first meeting each year.) The equivalent of the Greek god Zeus, Jupiter's chief symbols were the thunderbolt and the eagle. Besides Optimus Maximus, he had a number of different manifestations, among them Divis pater (Father of Heaven), Fugurator (Sender of Lightning), Invictus (Invincible), Latialis (Leader of the Latin Feast), Prodigialialis (Sender of Omens), and Triumphator (Victor). Each had its special characteristics, worshipers, and temples.

*Jupiter and his two chief symbols: the eagle and the thunderbolt.*

Aeneas than she had been before, Dido implored him to stay with her and make Carthage the new home he sought. And for a while, it looked as though the Trojan prince might forget about his prophesied Italian destiny and become the king of the North African kingdom she ruled.

However, mighty Jupiter did not desire for Aeneas to settle down in Carthage. The leader of the gods sent his messenger, the swift-footed Mercury, to remind Aeneas that he had a duty to future generations of Italians. "You forget, it seems, your true kingdom, your destiny!" Mercury told Aeneas (according to Virgil).

> Now Jove [another name for Jupiter] Almighty, the absolute monarch of the gods, has sent me, he who holds heaven and earth in the palm of his hand. . . . What are you doing? Why do you linger here in north Africa? If no ambition spurs you, nor desire to see yourself renowned for your own deeds, what about Ascanius [Aeneas's son]? The realm of Italy and the Roman inheritance are his due.[28]

Hearing this appeal, Aeneas came to his senses and made preparations to leave Carthage. Not surprisingly, Dido was both grief-stricken and angry that he would suddenly leave her this way; and despite her love for him, she hurled harsh words at him. "You traitor!" she screamed.

*Queen Dido listens to Aeneas tell the story of the fall of Troy.*

Did you hope to mask such treachery and silently slink from my land? Is there nothing to keep you? Nothing that my life or our love has given you, knowing that if you go, I cannot but die? . . . Oh God, I am driven raving mad with fury! . . . Go! Seek Italy on a tempest, seek your realms over the storm-crests, and I pray if the gods are as true to themselves as their powers that you will be smashed on the rocks, calling on Dido's name! [29]

Then she pronounced a terrible curse. May future Carthaginians and Aeneas's descendants always hate one another, she said. Let there be no treaties between the two peoples, and let generation after generation be consumed by weapons and war. (This curse was fulfilled, for hundreds of years later Carthage and Rome fought to the death in three bloody wars.)

## The Coming of the Master Race

After departing Africa, Aeneas sailed to Cumae in southern Italy. There, a prophet had earlier told him, he should seek out the Sibyl, a wise woman who could see into the future. The Sibyl greeted him and told him that he was destined to fight a war in Italy over the right to marry an Italian bride. He then begged her to help him find a way into the underworld so that he might once more see his beloved father, who had died during the journey across the Mediterranean. Granting the request, the Sibyl led Aeneas down into the underworld, and in time they found the spirit of old Anchises.

Following their joyful reunion, the father offered to show the son the future of the grand and blessed race Aeneas would sire. "Come then," said Anchises, "I shall show you the whole span of our destiny." First, he revealed, Aeneas's offspring would establish the city of Alba Longa in the Italian region of Latium (lying south of the Tiber River); and the line of Alba's noble rulers would lead to Romulus, who himself would establish a city—none other than Rome. "Under his tutelage," Anchises predicted, "our glorious Rome shall rule the whole wide world, and her spirit shall match the spirit of the gods." [30] Anchises showed his son the long line of noble Romans, finally culminating in the greatest of them all, Augustus Caesar, who was destined to bring about a new golden age for Rome and humanity. (Indeed, it was Augustus who established the Roman Empire.)

After Aeneas and the Sibyl returned from their journey through the lower regions, the hero traveled northward to Latium to fulfill the destiny that had been revealed to him. He met the local ruler, Latinus, and soon sought the hand of that king's daughter, Lavinia. But Turnus, prince of a neighboring people called the Rutulians, had already asked for Lavinia's hand, and the rivalry over Lavinia soon led to a terrible war, thus fulfilling the Sibyl's prophecy that Aeneas would fight over an Italian bride.

Eventually Aeneas defeated Turnus and married Lavinia. And from the union of the Trojan and Latin races, fulfilling the destiny ordained by Father Jupiter himself, sprang

# Helping to Define The Roman Identity

Romulus's welcoming of foreigners, like the non-Italian origins of Aeneas into his new city, were among attempts by later Romans to explain the cosmopolitan nature of their state. As noted scholar T. J. Cornell explains in this excerpt from his acclaimed book *The Beginnings of Rome:*

*The Roman foundation legend provides evidence, first and foremost, of how the Romans of later times chose to see themselves, and how they wished to be seen by others. The story carries a strong ideological message. The most revealing sign of this is the way it defines the identity of the Roman people as a mixture of different ethnic groups, and of Roman culture as the product of various foreign influences. There could hardly be a greater contrast with the foundation myths of the Greek cities, which insisted on the purity and continuity of their origins. . . . The Roman saga was characteristic of a people who had built up their power by extending their citizenship and continuously admitting new elements into their midst. From this point of view, we can appreciate the powerful appeal of the Aeneid, an epic poem that to this day retains a special significance for migrants and refugees. Rome was also unique among ancient societies in its practice of assimilating freed slaves, who automatically became Roman citizens on manumission [gaining their freedom].*

the lineage of the noble Romans, who would one day rule all the world. For the Romans, Jupiter had earlier told the love goddess Venus, "I see no measure nor date and I grant them dominion without end. . . . Even Juno will mend her ways and vie with me in cherishing the Romans, the master race, the wearers of the toga."[31]

## The Survival of Romulus and Remus

In the years that followed, the Sibyl's prophecy came to pass as Aeneas's descendants established Alba Longa on the Latium plain. Eventually two new members of the royal house of that noble city were born—Romulus and his twin brother, Remus. Their great-uncle

Amulius, who usurped the throne from their grandfather Numitor when they were still infants, ordered them to be drowned in the Tiber. But they fortunately washed ashore, where a she-wolf fed them and some poor shepherds eventually took them in. When the brothers grew to manhood and learned their true identities, they returned to Alba, overthrew Amulius, and restored Numitor, the rightful king, to his throne. Then they set out to establish a new city of their own on the northern edge of the Latium plain.

As it turned out, however, Romulus ended up founding the city by himself, for he and Remus got into a petty squabble, fought, and Romulus slew his brother. According to Livy's account:

Romulus and Remus were suddenly seized by an urge to found a new settlement on the spot where they had been left to drown as infants and had been subsequently brought up. . . . Unhappily, the brothers' plans for the future were marred by the same source which had divided their grandfather and Amulius—jealousy and ambition. A disgraceful quarrel arose from a matter in itself trivial. As the brothers were twins and all questions of seniority were therefore precluded, they determined to ask the gods of the countryside to declare by augury [divine signs revealed in the actions of birds] which of them should govern the new town once it was founded, and give his name to it. . . . Remus, the story goes, was the first to receive a sign—six vultures [in some accounts, eagles]; and no sooner was this made known to the people than double the number of birds appeared to Romulus. The followers of each promptly saluted their masters as king. . . . Angry words ensued, followed all too soon by blows, and in the course of the fray Remus was killed. There is another story, a commoner one, according to which Remus, by way of jeering at his brother, jumped over the half-built walls of the new settlement, whereupon Romulus killed him in a fit of rage, adding the threat, "So perish whoever else shall overleap my battlements." This, then, was how Romulus obtained the sole power. The newly built city was called by its founder's name.[32]

The Capitoline Wolf, *a bronze Etruscan sculpture from around 500 B.C., depicts the legend of the she-wolf suckling the twins Romulus and Remus.*

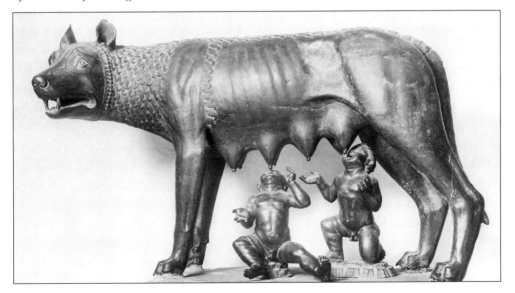

# Birthday of a Great Country

Shortly after Remus's tragic death, Romulus regretted what had happened and with great sorrow buried his brother. Then he proceeded to lay the new town's initial foundations. Realizing that he needed help, he sent for masons, workers, and advisers from Etruria (now known as Tuscany, the homeland of a highly civilized Italian people, the Etruscans). They instructed him in the proper steps one had to follow to construct a city and the accepted religious ceremonies that should be conducted to inaugurate it. "First," Plutarch wrote in his *Life of Romulus*,

*A portrait of Romulus, the founder of Rome.*

> they dug a round trench . . . and into it solemnly threw the first-fruits of all things either good by custom or necessary by nature; lastly, every man taking a small piece of earth of the country from whence he came, they all threw [the pieces] in randomly together. Making this trench . . . their center, they laid out the boundary of the city in a circle round it. Then the founder fitted to a plow a metal plowshare [blade], and, yoking together a bull and a cow, drove himself a deep line or furrow round the boundary.[33]

Using this line in the dirt as a guide, Romulus and the others laid out the city's outer defensive wall around the Palatine, one of the seven low hills on which, over time, Rome would rise. This auspicious day when the eternal city's foundations were laid was the twenty-first of April. Future generations of Romans would keep that day holy by making it an annual holiday, calling it their country's birthday. No living creature was allowed to be sacrificed on that holiday, for all wanted to celebrate their country's founding in a pure way, without the shedding of blood.

Once he had established Rome, Romulus proceeded immediately to deal with some important religious, legal, and social matters. According to Livy:

> Having performed with proper ceremony his religious duties, he summoned his subjects and gave them

laws, without which the creation of a unified people and government would not have been possible. . . . Meanwhile Rome was growing. . . . To help fill his big new town, [Romulus] threw open . . . a place of asylum for fugitives. Hither fled for refuge all the outcasts from the neighboring peoples; some free, some slaves, and all of them wanting nothing more than a fresh start. That mob was the first real addition to the city's strength, the first step toward her future greatness.[34]

## Courage and Honor in the Face of Danger

Thanks to the efforts of Romulus and his immediate successors, Rome continued to grow larger and stronger. Its public buildings and houses came to cover the seven hills and the valleys between them, and the territory under its rule expanded ever outward. This expansion naturally brought the Romans into conflict with various neighboring peoples who increasingly saw Rome as a threat to their own stability. Among these enemies, for instance, were the Etruscans, who had once been on friendly terms with the Romans. Time after time, Etruscan and other foreign armies threatened the Roman state; and a number of Roman commanders and defenders earned lasting reputations as heroes for saving their country from destruction.

Among the most famous of these early Roman heroes were Horatius Cocles and Lucius Quinctius Cincinnatus. Horatius rose to fame at the time that Lars Porsenna, king of the powerful Etruscan city of Clusium, led a mighty army against Rome. Seeing the approach of the Etruscans, thousands of Roman farmers abandoned their homes and fled into the city. The few Roman troops then stationed in the countryside also panicked and joined the civilians in their flight, which allowed Porsenna's army to approach the Sublician, the wooden bridge leading across the Tiber and into the heart of the city. The man guarding the bridge at that moment was none other than Horatius. In Livy's words, he was "that great soldier whom the fortune of Rome gave to be her shield on that day of peril."[35]

As the last of the fleeing Roman troops crossed the bridge, Horatius stopped them and asked what good it would do to retreat into the city. By abandoning their posts, he said, they had opened the way for the enemy to capture it. Horatius told them to do as he said and together they might yet save their homes and way of life. He ordered them to destroy the bridge behind him while he held off the approaching Etruscans. According to Livy:

> Proudly he took his stand at the outer edge of the bridge . . . sword and shield ready for action, preparing himself for close combat, one man against an army. The advancing enemy paused in sheer astonishment at such reckless courage. Two other men . . . were ashamed to leave Horatius alone, and with their support he won through the

*In this seventeenth century painting Horatius Cocles saves Rome at the Sublican bridge.*

first few minutes of desperate danger. Soon, however, he forced them to save themselves and leave him. ...Once more Horatius stood alone; with defiance in his eyes he confronted the Etruscans, challenging one after another to single combat.[36]

Eventually the lone defender's comrades succeeded in demolishing the bridge, which collapsed into the Tiber's raging waters, taking brave Horatius with it. To the enemy's amazement and the Romans' relief, moments later the hero's head appeared above the waves. He managed to swim to the safe shore while a shower of Etruscan spears and arrows rained down around him. The enemy

had no choice now but to withdraw, and the grateful Romans showed their gratitude for Horatius's daring rescue of Rome by erecting a statue of him in the city's main square.

Another Roman savior, Cincinnatus, who lived two generations after Horatius, was a poor, diligent farmer who had a reputation for great honor and humility as well as unusual fighting skill. One day he was digging some ditches on his modest three-acre farm, which lay to the west of the Tiber, when a large group of his countrymen approached. To his surprise, many were wearing togas bearing a purple stripe, indicating that they were senators. Cincinnatus asked why so many noble and powerful Roman leaders had bothered to trek all the way out to his humble farm.

The senators told Cincinnatus that a large army of Aequi, fierce tribesmen who lived northeast of Rome, was on its way to capture and destroy the city. Faced with this threat, the Senate had decided to appoint someone dictator, an officer who took complete charge of the state and defended it during a dire emergency. Cincinnatus had been chosen, they said, partly because he was a patriot and a strong military leader, but also because he was the least likely person to abuse the lofty powers that would be conferred on him.

Cincinnatus more than lived up to the senators' expectations and his own reputation. He promptly donned his armor, took charge of the army, and crushed the Aequi in battle. Then, as Livy said, he "resigned the office of dictator after holding it for only fifteen days, having originally accepted it for a period of six months." [37] Quietly, without hesitation, and with no ceremony or regrets,

## The Office of Dictator

The early Roman hero Cincinnatus became famous for his exemplary execution of the public office of dictator. Important during the years of the Roman Republic (509–30 B.C.), the dictatorship was conceived as a way to help the state survive a national emergency. During such an emergency, the consuls (two administrator-generals who served jointly) appointed a dictator on the recommendation of the Senate. The appointee held supreme military and judicial authority for a period of six months, after which he was expected to step down. The dictator's second in command was the master of the horse (magister equitum). Besides the legendary Cincinnatus, one of the most famous and effective dictators was Quintus Fabius Maximus, "the Delayer," who was instrumental in Rome's deliverance from the Carthaginian invader Hannibal in the Second Punic War (218–201 B.C.). In the political turmoil of the first century B.C., the office of dictator was frequently abused, and it was abolished altogether after Julius Caesar's assassination in 44 B.C.

A line drawing of Cincinnatus with his plowshare.

Cincinnatus returned to his farm, remaining ever after the perfect example of the modest, honorable, patriotic Roman man.

Horatius and Cincinnatus constituted, in a sense, the later links in a chain of heroes stretching backward through the centuries. Aeneas had become a hero through an adventurous quest that had given birth to the Romans; Romulus had earned his heroic reputation by founding the great city of Rome; and men like Horatius and Cincinnatus had courageously and selflessly defended that city and its way of life. Rome could not have asked for more from any of them.

# Chinese Heroes: Struggling to Survive in a Hostile World

The similarities between Chinese heroes and their Greco-Roman counterparts—strength, courage, determination, and so forth—are immediately apparent. Yet the differences between them are just as evident. The nature of these differences is not merely cultural—having to do with language, customs, and beliefs that are often unfamiliar to people living in Western countries. The stories of the ancient Chinese heroes tend to be shorter, more fragmented, and are not tied together into long narratives like Homer's *Iliad* or the *Metamorphoses*, a large collection of myths compiled by the first-century B.C. Roman poet Ovid. Ancient China had no Homer, Ovid, or comparable great myth-teller, at

least none whose name and works have survived. Indeed, *survival* appears to be the key term for understanding the sources of early Chinese mythology, heroic or otherwise. The fact is that only a small fraction of China's mythological tradition, which was probably originally very extensive and rich, has survived the ages.

There are two major reasons that a great deal of this tradition either disappeared or underwent significant alteration and distortion. The first reason came about in the wake of momentous political changes that swept the ancient Chinese sphere. The era lasting from about 480 to 221 B.C. in that region is referred to as the period of the Warring States, in which a large number of small and moderate-sized city-states and kingdoms continually fought among themselves. In 221 B.C. the westernmost of these states, ruled by the Ch'in (or Qin) dynasty—a strong, authoritarian group of rulers—launched large-scale military campaigns. And in short order, the Ch'in overran and consolidated the other states. Under the Ch'in, for the first time in history China became a unified empire with a central administration. And that concept of unity and central government proved long-lived, inspiring Chinese leaders in the many centuries that followed.

The problem was that the Ch'in viewed the survival of the literature and traditions of the states they had conquered as a threat to their supremacy. The main culprit in this regard was evidently Li Si, a minister of the Ch'in emperor Shi Huang Di. In 213 B.C. Li Si supposedly told his master:

> Your Majesty has brought about a great achievement and founded a glory that will last for ten thousand years. But narrow-minded scholars cannot understand this. . . . Only

*In this medieval painting the Chinese emperor orders his soldiers to burn books and execute scholars.*

the scholars fail to conform to the new trends and study the past in order to criticize the present. They cause doubts and misgivings among the peasantry. . . . They indulge in public debate and encourage the common people to believe their lies. This being so, if no action is taken, the imperial authority will be diminished. . . . This must be prevented.

Your servant proposes that the Histories, save that of the Ch'in, shall be burned. . . . Those who dare to discuss or comment on the ancient institutions and stories shall be put to death. . . . Only those books which deal with medicine, divination [reading the future through divine signs], and agriculture shall be allowed to survive.[38]

59

Unfortunately for posterity, the emperor agreed with Li Si and gave the order to burn the old books; in the process, some 460 scholars were executed on charges of concealing texts in an attempt to save them. A handful of books, which included a few myths, were indeed saved this way. But much was lost, and the full extent and nature of this material will never be known.

The second reason that China's original myths are few and fragmentary is that most of those that survived the great Ch'in book-burning were purposely altered to conform to current philosophical or religious ideas. The Ch'in fell from power in 202 B.C., and a new dynasty (family line of rulers), the Han, replaced them. To their credit, the Han set about restoring and reconstructing the lost texts. However, their process was highly selective and tailored to their own views and needs. On the one hand, says Derk Bodde, an expert on Chinese mythology, they were "always intensely interested in the search for historical precedents which would confirm their own social and political doctrines."[39]

On the other hand, the Han scholars tended to be rational in their worldview and often tried to explain away supernatural and fantastic concepts found in the old stories. Their view of ancient mythical characters was similar to that of the fourth-century B.C. Greek scholar Euhemerus. He held, probably correctly in large degree, that the ancient gods and heroes were originally human rulers and military leaders who over the course of time had come to be seen as far more powerful than they had actually been. The difference was that the Greeks and Romans did

not try to change their myths to conform to Euhemerus's view; whereas the Chinese scholars of the Han centuries did alter many of their own myths, changing some gods and monsters into ordinary people and giving them roles in newly written histories of previous Chinese eras. In short, while Greco-Roman myths changed historical people into mythical heroes, many Chinese histories portrayed mythical creatures and heroes as real. "The results," says Bodde, "have been disastrous for the preservation of early Chinese myths . . . [which] have either vanished entirely or suffered grievous distortion."[40]

## Kun and the Swelling Earth

Nevertheless, when stripped down to their core—their personalities, abilities, and larger-than-life accomplishments—a number of early Chinese heroes bear strong resemblance to their counterparts in Europe and the Near East. Like most heroes in these regions, Chinese heroes struggled to survive in a hostile, uncertain world and to bring security and/or order to that world. The story of Kun and Yü and their efforts to control the mighty floodwaters, perhaps the most famous and popular of all the Chinese myths, is a case in point.

Long ago in the days when the great emperor Yao ruled China, the story begins, a great flood came washing across the land. According to the ancient text known as *The Classic of History:*

> Everywhere the tremendous flood waters were wreaking destruction.

Spreading afar, they embraced the mountains and rose above the hills. In a vast flow, they swelled up to Heaven. The people below were groaning in despair.[41]

Fearing that the world and everyone living in it would be destroyed, Yao called on a former soldier named Kun for help. Tall and strong, Kun had a reputation for courage and fortitude. He immediately agreed to attempt to hold back the floodwaters.

With amazing power and speed, Kun gathered dirt from one of the few dry areas left on the earth's surface and used it to erect huge dams in the path of the waters. But even a hero as strong and resourceful as he could not make these dams large enough and strong enough in time to keep up with the rapidly rising waters. What could be done, Kun wondered, for as fast as he built the dams the water overflowed them. There had to be a way to build them faster and save the world and humanity from certain drowning. The question was how he could accomplish this feat.

At that moment, Kun's question was answered by a tortoise and a horned owl,

# Legends Based in Reality?

The myths of Kun and Yü and their heroic efforts to control the floodwaters and make the world habitable take place in a legendary bygone era that ends with Yü becoming the first ruler of the first Chinese dynasty, the Hsia (or Xia). The mythical rule of the Hsia may well have been based on a real early Chinese society, as explained here by former Columbia University scholar L. Carrington Goodrich (from his *Short History of the Chinese People*).

[According to] the scribes who penned traditional Chinese history during the first millennium before our era . . . the period of the Hsia . . . began, according to one document, in the year corresponding to 1994 B.C. and lasted to 1523 B.C. (Another document, not so generally supported by scholars, puts the first date at 2205 B.C.) During these five centuries, again according to tradition, a succession of princes ruled a group of city-states . . . near the last great bend of the Yellow River [in eastern China]. Their people knew the use of bronze weapons, went to war in chariots, engaged in agriculture . . . and put down their ideas in writing. Actually, there is no satisfactory evidence that this state existed; we cannot identify a single vessel or weapon or bronze inscription as being Hsia in date. Nevertheless, the many artifacts and inscriptions that have come down to us from the next historic period are not primitive in the least and must have had a history in China of several hundred years. They make us willing to grant that, even if the Hsia never existed, there were centers near the banks of the Yellow River which knew the art of casting bronze, learned the value of the silkworm, used the wheel on the farm and in war, and began to use written symbols. The first steps toward civilization had been taken.

which appeared seemingly out of nowhere. (Were they sent by a sympathetic god? No one knows.) The tortoise and the owl advised Kun to travel as swiftly as possible up to heaven, where a great god, Ti, possessed a special kind of dirt called the "swelling earth." The swelling earth had the magical ability to expand continually, they said; and if Kun used it to construct his dams, these barriers would grow in size and might keep pace with the rising waters.

Kun thought this was an excellent idea. He took the advice of the tortoise and owl and hurried up to heaven, where he had no trouble finding Ti's swelling earth. However, the hero was in such a hurry to save the world that he decided not to waste any time asking the god if it was all right to use some of the magical earth. Kun reasoned that the great Ti would understand Kun's urgent need for this magical earth. This assumption on Kun's part turned out to be a serious blunder, however. He was in the midst of building his first dam with the swelling earth when Ti, angry over what he saw as an outright theft of his property, intervened. Ti sent Chu Yung, the god of fire, to punish Kun. At a place called Feather Mountain, in a sunless region in China's far northern reaches, Chu Yung struck down and killed the well-meaning Kun. Then, according to an ancient text called *Questions of Heaven*, Kun "lay exposed on Feather Mountain for a long time. But why did he not decompose for three years?"[42]

## Yü Makes the Land Habitable

The answer to the question of why Kun's body did not rot away, as mortal bodies always do, was answered at the end of the three years. Someone (whose identity remains unknown) came along and saw the corpse lying there. Drawing his sword, the passerby slit open Kun's belly and a remarkable miracle occurred: Out popped the fully grown Yü, Kun's son and himself an even greater warrior and hero than his father had been! Thus, the reason that Kun's body had not decomposed was that it was sustaining the growth of Yü inside.

Yü was so concerned about the floodwaters—which had continued to rise over the three years and by now covered most of the world—that he immediately accepted the task of completing his father's unfinished work. Yü declared that he would save humanity from destruction and in the process make the land habitable again so that the people would have a place to live and grow their food. Furthermore, he would take steps to ensure that in the future no world-covering flood would be possible. He swore on his honor to devote himself to these tasks.

With no thought for his own comfort or desires, the noble and unselfish young hero set about his daunting task. He dug channels that ran for miles along the earth's surface, making them so deep that the floodwaters began to drain into them, carrying excess water into the rivers and from there into the open seas. He also heaped up gigantic mounds of earth, fashioning dams across the

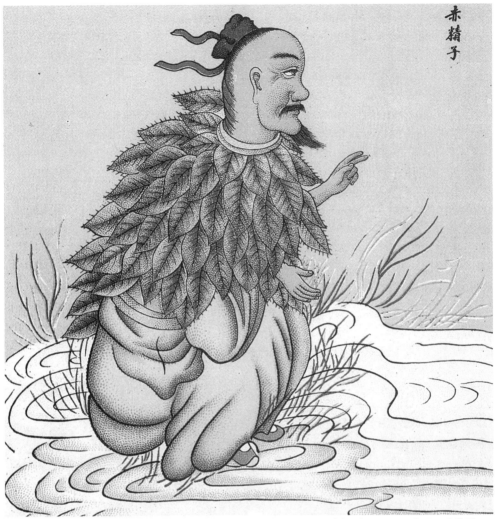

*A painting of the Chinese god of fire, Chu Yung, who was ordered by the great god Ti to kill Kun.*

countryside. These blocked the underground springs that were the source of the floodwaters; there were 233,559 of them in all, but this huge number did not intimidate Yü, who plugged them up one by one. He also erected and shaped towering mountains at the world's boundaries to serve as anchors to keep the land between them from washing away. As told in the ancient texts:

The Nine Provinces [i.e., the nine regions of China] were standardized. The four quarters [i.e., four corners of the earth] were made habitable. The Nine Mountains were deforested and put down for arable land. The sources of the Nine Rivers were dredged. The Nine Marshes were banked up. The Four Seas had their concourses opened freely. . . . All the soils were compared and classified. Their land values and revenues were carefully controlled. [43]

These incredible accomplishments took Yü ten years, a period during which he labored ceaselessly. He had a family (the relatives of his father, Kun) and passed by their house each day on his way to build a dam or create a mountain. But he was so dedicated to completing his task that he never once stopped to visit them. His work was so difficult and relentless, in fact, that his fingernails wore away and part of his body, including one leg, shriveled so that he walked with a severe limp; later, people came to call it "the Yü walk."

Finally, after the last of his labors were completed, Yü was able to rest and visit his family. Not long afterward, he established China's first hereditary dynasty, the Hsia (or Xia), serving as its first and most illustrious ruler. And ever after, people looked on him as their savior and a hero of the greatest stature. As a later Chinese nobleman remarked: "Were it not for Yü, all of us would be fish!" [44]

## The Coming of the Lord of the Granary

Another Chinese hero who overcame natural forces and obstacles, as well as human ones, was Wu-hsiang, better known as the Lord of the Granary. He did not start out as a lord or an important person in any sense, but

*Kun Mountain, on the India-China border, is so named in honor of the Chinese hero Kun.*

# The Origins of Rice

The myth of the Lord of the Granary is only one of many early Chinese legends that incorporate the theme of agriculture, which is not surprising considering how essential crop production was (and still is) in sustaining life in China. In fact, the Chinese had several myths explaining the origins of specific crops. In this excerpt from his *Chinese Mythology*, noted scholar Anthony Christie retells two of those dealing with rice, a Chinese staple food.

*The rice plant existed from the beginning but its ears were not filled. This was the time when people lived by hunting and gathering. The goddess Guan Yin saw that people lived in hardship and near starvation. She was moved to pity and resolved to help them. She went secretly into the rice fields and squeezed her breasts so that the milk flowed into the ears of the rice plants. Almost all of them were filled, but to complete her task she had to press so hard that a mixture of milk and blood flowed into the plants. That is why there are two kinds of rice, the white from the milk, the red from the mixture of milk and blood. In another story, rice is the gift of a dog. After the floods had been controlled by Yü, people found that all the old plants had been destroyed, but that no new ones had taken their place. So they had to live by hunting. One day a dog was seen to emerge from a waterlogged field. From its tail there hung branches of yellow ears full of seeds, which people planted in the wet, but drained fields. The seeds grew and the plants ripened to give the people rice. For this they were very grateful to the dog, so before eating they always offered a little food to the dog and at the first meal after the rice harvest the food was shared with the dog.*

rather earned fame and power by virtue of his strength, courage, and daring. He was born in the region inhabited by the Pa clan (modern Szechwan, in south-central China) in the dim past when no chieftains yet ruled over the people; instead, the local inhabitants were subject to the whims of various local gods and spirits, some of them beneficial, others selfish and unkindly.

Over the years, through his honesty, cunning, and fighting skill, Wu-hsiang earned a name for himself among the members of his clan. His superior attributes turned out to be useful and fortunate, both to them and to himself; for there eventually came a time

when the Pa began to compete with other neighboring clans, including the Fan, Shen, Hsiang, and Cheng, each hoping to be the first clan to rule all of the humans in the region. The Pa sent Wu-hsiang to engage in a series of contests with the champions of the other clans. According to the ancient text known as *The Origin of Hereditary Families*, these champions

all competed for divine power to rule. They all together threw their swords at a rock and agreed that whoever could hit the target would be elevated to become their lord. When the son of the Pa clan, Wu-hsiang, was the only one to hit the target, the other contestants all sighed heavily. [Proposing another test, Wu-hsiang] ordered each clan to sail in an earthenware boat, carved with designs and painted, and to float the boats in the river. They made an agreement that whoever could stay afloat would become their lord. The boats of the other clans all sank into the waters, and Wu-hsiang's was the only one to stay afloat. So they unanimously made him their chieftain.[45]

On becoming the leader of the clans, Wu-hsiang became known as the Lord of the Granary, perhaps because he now had authority over the farmers and farmlands that grew the food for all the clans.

Not long after becoming leader of the people, Wu-hsiang decided that they needed a fine and proper city in which to live, for up to that time they had known only small, poor villages. Searching for just the right place to establish his new city, he sailed his earthenware boat downstream for many miles. Eventually he reached a sharp bend in the river and saw tall rocky cliffs rising above him. Suddenly one of the cliffs collapsed, making a frightful noise and sending fragments of stone flying in all directions. For reasons known only to himself, Wu-hsiang decided that this would be a good place to found his city, so he climbed up the jagged pile of rocks until he stood at the summit. There he found a flat rock and sat on it. He decided that he would

make a new home for himself there, and so he erected a house beside the rock. In the months and years that followed, hundreds and then thousands of people followed his example and built their own houses there.

## The Salt Goddess Blots Out the Sun

Wu-hsiang's next adventure brought him into conflict with one of the local gods that had for so long affected the lives of the humans in the region. Beyond the farmlands of the clans stretched a large expanse of territory filled with rich soil, plentiful deposits of salt (needed for preserving as well as for seasoning food), and numerous streams stocked with all kinds of fish. This territory was still under the control of the Goddess of the Salt River. She did not want her domain to fall into the hands of the clans; moreover, she was selfish and not very neighborly, refusing to trade her salt, fish, and other products for their goods.

Wu-hsiang was sure that he could defeat the goddess and secure these valuable lands; so he journeyed to the Salt River in his earthenware boat. The goddess saw him coming and went out, dressed in her finest clothes, to meet him. Though humans usually did not impress her, she immediately saw that this stranger was no ordinary person. Taken with his handsome looks and heroic stature, she made him an offer, saying that the land was vast and well stocked with fruit, fish, and salt, so the man should stay there and live with her from now on. She promised that he would be very comfortable and want for nothing. Of course, the noble

Wu-hsiang had no intention of abandoning his people to live in luxury with this divine being, and he flatly refused her offer.

Needless to say, the goddess was insulted and angry at being rejected by a mere mortal. That night, as Wu-hsiang slept, she crept up on him and waited quietly. The next morning, as he was awakening, she changed herself into a large insect and summoned millions of other insects, creating a huge swarm that filled the sky. The swarm was so large and dense, in fact, that it blotted out the sunlight and the land became pitch-black. "The Lord of the Granary could not make out which was east or west for seven days and seven nights," [46] says the ancient text. From horizon to horizon, all agriculture and other food production came to a standstill and the people began to starve.

Finally Wu-hsiang hatched a daring plan to outwit the goddess and save the people. He called on the goddess to change herself back into her normal form because he had an important message for her. He had decided that he had been foolish to refuse her generous offer, he told her after she had retaken her usual form. And he would stay there with her forever, just as she desired. The goddess stared at him warily. It was a most wise decision, she said. But how could she be sure of the man's sincerity? Was it not customary to seal a bargain with a gift? she asked. The crafty Wu-hsiang had anticipated such a question, and he was ready with a clever answer. He pleaded with her to accept his offer of a beautiful belt made of green silk, saying that it was the least he could do to repay her kindness and generosity.

The goddess was so bedazzled by the gift the man had given her that she fell for the ploy. She put on the belt and gazed admiringly at herself in a mirror, thereby lowering her guard. Wu-hsiang swiftly took advantage of the situation. Leaping up onto a nearby rock, he pulled out his mighty bow, took aim, and let loose one arrow after another, all of which found their marks in the goddess's body. A few moments later she lay dead; and almost immediately the insect swarm dissipated and the sky cleared. When Wu-hsiang returned to the great city of Yi, the people rejoiced and congratulated him on his victory, which has remained legendary ever since.

## The Brides of the River God

Wu-hsiang was certainly not the only hero to do battle with divine forces. A brave, clever, and resourceful soldier-administrator named Li Ping also became famous for defending his people against the threatening behavior of a local river god. Several centuries after the defeat of the Goddess of the Salt River, the Ch'in gained control of a large portion of China. One of the Ch'in rulers, King Chao Hsiang, asked Li Ping to take charge of a territory recently conquered by the Ch'in. And, considering it an honor to be asked, the goodly and patriotic Li Ping accepted the job.

When Li Ping arrived at his new post, he was disturbed to learn that the local inhabitants had long been plagued by a mean-spirited god who lived in the river that flowed near the local capital. Every year the god demanded that the people deliver to him two young maidens, whom he dragged down into the depths of the river. Supposedly they were to be his brides. But some people believed that he killed and ate the poor girls. Whatever their ultimate fate might be, there was no doubt that once the maidens disappeared beneath the river's surface, they were never seen again.

Unlike the locals, Li Ping was not frightened by the river god. And the new administrator was not about to allow those under his care and guidance to continue being terrorized by the creature. When the god made his next demand for the delivery of his "brides," Li Ping told the people to keep their daughters at home and let him handle the situation. Li Ping summoned his own

*Located in Xian, China, this sculpture celebrates the emperor Chín unifying China. The Chín's rule was disastrous for the preservation of early Chinese myths.*

# The Five Strongmen

Some of the heroes described in the various surviving fragments of early Chinese myths were little more than characters invented to explain the existence of natural artifacts and phenomena. The fragment presented here (quoted by Anne Birrell in her book *Chinese Mythology*), for instance, attributes the origin of some large vertical stones to five heroic strongmen.

*In the reign of Emperor K'ai-ming . . . there were in Shu five strongmen who could move mountains and lift weights of three hundred thousand pounds. Every time a prince passed away, they would immediately set up a huge stone thirty feet long, weighing thirty thousand pounds, for the tomb's memorial stone. Today, these are like stalagmites [mineral deposits that rise in vertical columns from the floor of a cave]. The area is called the Stalagmite Village.*

two daughters and dressed them in their finest outfits. They asked him where they were going, and he answered that he was taking them down to the river to meet the god who lived there. The girls had heard about what happened to the maidens who were sent to be the god's brides and they became fearful. But Li Ping reassured them. As long as they did exactly as he instructed, he said, no harm would come to them.

Having said that, Li Ping led his young daughters to the riverbank and called out to the god. He asked the being to show itself, for the man had brought the yearly brides it had demanded. When the god, who looked like a big, hairy, ugly man, appeared, he gave Li Ping a questioning look. He demanded to know who the man was, for the god had never seen him before. Li Ping replied that he was the new local administrator and that he had come to fulfill the god's demand and also to offer him a humble gift—some wine. Li Ping invited the god to drink with him to

celebrate the impending marriage to the maidens.

But the river god had no interest in wine or any other gift, for all he could think about at that moment was seizing the girls and dragging them to their doom. When he refused to drink, just as Li Ping had expected he would, the man stepped forward and addressed him sternly. The god's refusal to drink the wine offered to him was a breach of common manners and civility, the man said. The being had therefore insulted and mocked Li Ping and must now fight him before he could lay claim to the girls.

Thinking that fighting and killing a mere human would be easy, the god lunged forward and the two joined in battle. (Some accounts say that they changed themselves into huge blue oxen and locked horns; but it is more likely that they fought as men did in those days, with swords.) To his surprise, the river god found that he was no match for Li Ping, who was a powerful, quick-moving, and highly skilled swordsman. The god eventually grew tired and faltered, lowering his weapon just enough for the man to find an opening. And with a tremendous thrust, Li Ping sank his sword deep in his opponent's guts. Groaning loudly, the river god collapsed into a heap and soon the shade of death darkened his eyes.

Thanks to the stalwart Li Ping, the people no longer had to suffer the fear and sorrow of losing their beloved daughters. He had not saved the world, as Yü had. Nor had he founded a great city, as in the case of Wu-hsiang. Instead, like a number of heroes before and after him, Li Ping exemplified that rare individual who possesses the courage, wit, and determination to buy freedom for the oppressed.

# Celtic Heroes: Feasting and Fighting in an Ideal World

The mythology of the ancient Celts is an unusually heroic one. In fact, in the sheer number of heroes it contains and the manner in which these characters are depicted, Celtic mythology rivals and in some ways resembles ancient Greek mythology. To understand why the Celts had such a strong heroic tradition, one must first come to grips with who these fascinating people were and the unique nature of their religious and other traditions.

The Celts were originally a seminomadic tribal people. Among the most important and prolific of Europe's early inhabitants, they spread across large portions of the continent between 1200 and 100 B.C. At the maximum extent of their influence, between around 400 and 200 B.C., they occupied Ireland and Britain, most of France and Spain, and large portions of central Europe stretching eastward to the western shore of the Black Sea. They naturally came into frequent contact with the Greeks and Romans, who inhabited and controlled southern Europe. (The Greeks called them *Keltoi*, the Romans *Celtae*.) And because the Celts had no cities, preferring a pastoral existence dominated by simple farms and villages, the Greco-Roman world viewed them as barbarians. In reality, though they were less advanced materially speaking than the Greeks and Romans, the Celts were no less civilized; they had laws, considerable social organization, and rich, well-developed religious traditions.

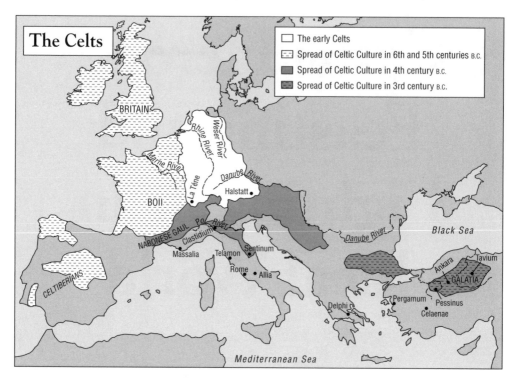

**The Celts**

- ☐ The early Celts
- ⊡ Spread of Celtic Culture in 6th and 5th centuries B.C.
- ▨ Spread of Celtic Culture in 4th century B.C.
- ▦ Spread of Celtic Culture in 3rd century B.C.

BRITAIN

Weser River
Rhine River
Marne River
Danube River
La Tène
Halstatt
BOII
NABONESE GAUL
Po River
Clastidium
Massalia
Telamon
Sentinum
Rome
Allia
Danube River
Black Sea
CELTIBERIANS
Delphi
Pergamum
Pessinus
Celaenae
Ankara
Tavium
GALATIA
Mediterranean Sea

Another strike against the Celts from the Greco-Roman viewpoint was their lack of written literature, which had a direct bearing on how their myths were eventually transmitted to later ages. Because they were for a long time illiterate, the Celts did not record their traditions, myths, laws, and other ideas. So the original Celtic myths were passed from generation to generation by word of mouth. The first literary references to the Celts and to Celtic gods and myths were those of the classical Greek and Roman writers. Their narratives are fascinating and important, but since these writers were obviously biased by their contempt for the "barbarians" and their "primitive" ways, they often present a distorted view of their subjects. As Miranda J. Green of the University of Wales, Cardiff, puts it:

Classical commentators on the Celts were witnesses to a set of traditions and thought-processes which were alien to them. . . . [Therefore] the Mediterranean authors selected and sensationalized aspects of [Celtic religion] which they felt would fit the image of a primitive people, beyond the edge of the civilized world. Certainly the picture painted by these writers is very fragmentary . . . and Celtic religion is frequently perceived according to the framework of the Greco-Roman world.[47]

More important written sources of Celtic mythology are those that were composed in the early Irish and Welsh tongues from roughly the sixth through the twelfth centuries. Although these sources are much more informative and reliable than the Greco-Roman ones, they also present some formidable problems. First, they contain mainly the legends of the Celts of that region and so leave out the surely extensive and rich lore of the rest of Celtic Europe. Second, they were written during the medieval Christian age that directly followed the disintegration of the classical Greco-Roman world. Many of the compilers were Christian monks who felt obliged to make many of the old pagan myths more "acceptable" to Christian readers; so they often reduced pagan gods to human historical figures or presented the myths as collections of childish superstitions rather than as integral facets of a different and equally worthy religious system.

As for that religion, it was polytheistic, like that of the Greeks and Romans. But unlike the Greeks and Romans, the Celts often pictured their gods as their own distant ancestors rather than as their creators. This made these deities in large degree interchangeable with human heroes. According to historian Peter B. Ellis, a noted authority on the Celts and their history:

> The Celts made their heroes into gods and their gods into heroes. In the lives of these gods and heroes, the lives of the people and the essence of their religious traditions were mirrored. Celtic heroes . . . were totally human and were subject to all the natural virtues and

vices. . . . Yet their world was one of rural happiness, a world in which they indulged in all the pleasures of moral life in an idealized form: love of nature, art, games, feasting, hunting, and heroic single-handed combat.[48]

In this idealized heroic world of godlike men, immortality was an accepted fact. Most Celts evidently believed that when people died in this world, they were reborn in another, better one; when they died in that world, they were reborn once more in this one; and this process was repeated in an endless cycle.

The final category of sources for Celtic mythology is also problematic. It consists of a number of Welsh and English romances, such as the English (or Welsh) chronicler Geoffrey of Monmouth's *History of the Kings of Britain*, which mentions King Arthur, and the anonymous fourteenth-century poem *Sir Gawain and the Green Knight*. Much of the content of these works is current fiction supplied by the authors. Nevertheless, Arthur, Gawain, and other characters, as well as some of the situations, were drawn from or based on the old Celtic myths; so these later romantic tales, though far from primary sources, are often viewed as an extension of Celtic tradition.

## The Remarkable Boy

One of the greatest of all the many heroes of that tradition was Cuchulainn, the magnificent champion of Ulster, then the region encompassing most of northern Ireland. He is

*In this nineteenth century painting, Cuchulainn journeys to Emain Macha, to visit King Conchobhar.*

fame are a power forever."[49] And in fact, when he was but a child, a priest delivered a prophecy warning that the hero was destined to have a glorious but short life.

Cuchulainn was born with the name of Setanta. His mother was Dechtire (or Deichtine), daughter of Cathbad, high priest and adviser to Ulster's king, Conchobhar Mac Nessa. Some accounts say that King Conchobhar was Setanta's father; while others hold that Dechtire traveled to the otherworld (the invisible realm where the gods and bygone heroes lived) and coupled with Lug, the sun god, thereby producing Setanta. Whoever the boy's father really was, Dechtire was married to a man named Sualtam Mac Roth. And when she gave birth to the child, her husband accepted and raised him as his own. It is said that at the very moment of the birth, two beautiful twin foals were born nearby. These later became the hero's mighty and faithful chariot horses—the Grey of Macha and the Black of Saingliu.

sometimes called the "Irish Achilles" in reference to the central character and mighty warrior of the Greek Homer's epic poem, *Iliad*. Like Achilles, Cuchulainn died young and believed that it was far more important to accomplish great deeds and achieve eternal fame than to live a long but undistinguished life. "I care not if I last but a day," the Irish hero is credited with saying, "if my name and my

As the child grew, his heroic qualities quickly became apparent. By the time he was four years old, he already possessed the strength and stamina of a strong adult man. The young Setanta also possessed a grown man's ambition. Not long before his fifth birthday, he decided that he could wait no longer to prove his unusual abilities. Leaving his home in the countryside, he journeyed to Ulster's capital, Emain Macha, where Conchobhar held court.

Setanta had heard about that king's corps of 150 privileged boys, who lived in special quarters near the palace and there trained to someday become royal officers and champions. Carrying his club, ball, and spear, the youngster arrived to find the boys engaged in games on the royal athletic field. He attempted to join in the game, but the youths taunted him and some threw rocks and other missiles in an attempt to drive him away. Clearly, they had no inkling of whom

they were provoking. To the surprise of both the boys and their teachers, Setanta fearlessly grappled with the young men, wrestling three and four at a time and defeating all 150 in short order.

When King Conchobhar heard what had happened, he was astounded. He decided to keep this remarkable boy at Emain Macha and train him to become Ulster's champion. The realm needed as many great warriors as it could find, for it was frequently at war with Connaught (or Cannacht), the kingdom bordering it to the southwest. Moreover, in time it became clear that the boy was the only Ulsterman who was unaffected by a terrible curse that the war goddess

# Cuchulainn Undergoes Symbolic Initiation

In this excerpt from his book *Celtic Mythology*, scholar Proinsias Mac Cana explores the mythic symbolism of some of Cuchulainn's exploits.

*[In] his first warlike exploit . . . he seeks out and slays the three fearsome sons of [the water god] Nechtan, who have slaughtered as many Ulstermen as remain alive. . . . [On his return to Emain Macha, Cuchulainn is still in the throes of his fighting frenzy.] To ward off his fury, which does not discriminate between friend and foe, the Ulsterwomen . . . go forth naked to meet him. He hides his face in confusion and is immediately seized by the warriors and plunged successively into three vats of cold water. . . . When he has been restored by this treatment to a state of reason, he is clothed by the queen in a blue cloak and admitted . . . to the royal household. The incidents in this sequence reflect substantially the scenario of heroic initiation as it is found throughout the world. . . . The fight with the three sons of Nechtan belongs to the recurrent . . . theme of the hero's encounter with a trio of adversaries or with a three-headed monster. The intervention of the women has analogies in Celtic and other traditions and is evidently a ritual act. . . . The concept of the hero as one who is fired with an ardent fury belongs to a widespread notion that sacred power is marked by an intense accession of physical heat.*

Macha had inflicted on the realm several years before. Whenever Ulster faced a serious crisis, for five days its men became weak and suffered from severe pain and therefore could not fight.

An incident that gave the king great confidence in Setanta's abilities was one in which the boy earned his more familiar name of Cuchulainn. One day when the child was about seven years old, Culann, Ulster's mighty blacksmith, was giving a party for the king. Setanta was invited but arrived late. As he approached the palace gate, Culann's huge, ferocious guard dog attacked him and he responded by seizing the animal and slamming its head against some rocks. Culann strongly objected to the slaying of the hound as he, the king, and several others approached. Now, Culann complained, his sheep and chickens would be left unguarded. The boy raised a hand to calm him and pledged that he would take the hound's place and guard the man's herds and flocks until he had time to train another guard dog. Culann was satisfied with this arrangement. And from that day forward, people referred to the young hero as Cuchulainn, meaning "the Hound of Culann."

## Cuchulainn Saves the Realm

As time went on, Cuchulainn proved his valor and fighting prowess time and again. In his very first battle against adult warriors, he revealed a bizarre and frightening quality that he alone possessed, one that made him seem almost invincible in a fight. Called by various names, including the "frenzy" and the "warp-spasm," it was an incredible physical transformation. Noted mythologist Arthur Cotterell describes it this way:

> His body trembled violently; his heels and calves appeared in front; one eye receded into his head, the other stood out huge and red on his cheek; a man's head could fit into his jaw; his hair bristled like hawthorn, with a drop of blood at the end of each single hair; and from the top of his head arose a thick column of dark blood like the mast of a ship.[50]

While in this frenzied state, Cuchulainn's body spun around within his skin, and he let loose a terrifying howl that caused all the local spirits to howl along with him. Needless to say, the sight and sounds of the attack of this one-of-a-kind warrior struck terror into the hearts of his opponents; they either fled before him or died horribly as he beheaded them with his razor-sharp sword. On many a day the people of Ulster hurried to stand on the battlements atop the city's walls and watch their hero returning home on his shining chariot, carrying the blood-dripping heads of their enemies.

Eventually, however, when the hero was just seventeen years old, the priest's prophecy that his life would be short came to pass. Medb, queen of Connaught, had grown increasingly distressed at losing so many of her fine young warriors to the sword of Ulster's champion. She also wanted to lay her hands on the Brown Bull of Cualnge, which was said to possess semidivine or magical properties; this unusual creature was corralled in Ulster. So Medb raised the largest army ever seen in Ireland and marched on Ulster. Just as she had hoped, this threw Ulster into a crisis, invoking Macha's curse and causing all of the Ulstermen except Cuchulainn to abstain from battle for five days. Cuchulainn was indeed a formidable warrior, she told her advisers. But he was still only one man. And even he would not be able to defeat an army so large. Therefore, victory would surely be theirs.

Medb had severely underestimated Cuchulainn's resolve and raw courage, however. When the enemy attacked, he flew into his dreaded frenzy; and he killed them by the hundreds on day after day, though each day he grew a little weaker from the large

*Celtic Queen Medb severely underestimated Cuchulainn's resolve, raw courage, and skill.*

number of wounds he sustained. Near the end of the fifth day, Cuchulainn realized that all he needed to do was hold off Medb's forces for a few more hours. After that, Ulster's own mighty forces would be released from the effects of the curse and be able to launch a great counterattack. Limping and bleeding, the hero tied himself to a large upright stone to ensure that he would meet the enemy standing and fight to his last breath. This he

did. The men of Connaught fell before his sword for hours, as he chanted over and over: "My skill in arms grows great. On cowering enemies I let fall great blows. On entire armies I wage war in order to crush them!"[51]

Despite Cuchulainn's extraordinary strength and desperate courage, however, his opponents finally won out by virtue of their sheer numbers. As the mighty hero's life slipped away, Morrigan, goddess of death, took the form of a crow and landed on his shoulder; seeing this, some of Medb's soldiers rushed forward and cut off Cuchulainn's head and right hand. Their triumph was short-lived, however, for mere minutes later Ulster's warriors, freed from the curse, burst upon the scene and routed the invaders. Cuchulainn had saved the

*A famous statue of the dying Cuchulainn. Morrigan, the goddess of death, takes the form of a crow and perches on his shoulder.*

realm from disaster. And in doing so, he had earned what he had always desired most—eternal fame.

## The Betrayal of Finn MacCool

Another famous and fondly remembered Celtic hero, Finn MacCool (or Fionn MacCumal), lived in a legendary age when all of Ireland was ruled by one great king. Finn was the leader of a band of roving warriors known as the Fianna (or Fenians), who had pledged to defend Ireland's throne against all enemies. Membership in the group was a very special privilege and was only granted to the finest, bravest warriors, who had to undergo some fiendishly difficult initiations. According to Celtic mythologist Proinsias Mac Cana, the would-be member

was armed with a shield and a hazel stick and placed standing up to his waist in a hole in the ground, and nine warriors cast their spears at him simultaneously. If he suffered hurt thereby, he was not accepted into the Fianna. Next, his hair was braided and he was made to run through the woods of Ireland pursued at a brief interval by all the warriors. If he was overtaken and wounded, he was not accepted. Moreover, if

# Magic and Enchantment in Celtic Myth

The magic spell cast by Grainne on Diarmuid and the curse placed on Culhwch by his stepmother are only two of the many examples of magic and supernatural elements in Celtic mythology, as explained here by Arthur Cotterell, of London's Kingston College, from his *Celtic Mythology*.

*Enchantment permeates [runs throughout] Celtic myth, shrouding the tales in a haunting, dreamlike quality. The all-pervasive Otherworld lies behind much of the mystery and magic, penetrating the forests and lakes, and crafting charmed rings and weapons. Yet spells and magic also arose in the visible world where bards, druids [Celtic priests], and some privileged heroes, such as Finn MacCool, possessed magical powers. Bards could weaken the enemy with satire or enchanted sleep, while druids bewitched the host with magical illusions. Off the battlefield, love and romance were also subject to spells . . . or magical trickery. . . . On the brighter side, many heroes enjoyed the gifts of the Otherworld, such as Arthur's sword, Excalibur . . . and countless heroes were nourished or reborn from magical cauldrons. Miraculous cauldrons feature as a recurrent motif [theme] in Celtic myth. Some overflow with plenty, others restore the dead to life, while still others contain a special brew of wisdom. . . . Similar mystery bowls or cups feature in Greek and eastern myths as holy vessels of spiritual insight. Ultimately, the early Celtic cauldrons find expression in the Arthurian Grail [the cup used by Christ in the Last Supper], which overflows with spiritual sustenance and leads the hero from death to immortality.*

his weapons had quivered in his hand, if his hair had been disturbed by a hanging branch or if a dead branch had cracked under his foot, then neither was he accepted.[52]

Not surprisingly, such arduous tests ensured that Finn's followers were champions of the highest possible caliber.

Perhaps the most famous of Finn's exploits was his love for a fair lady, Grainne, and his rivalry for her with one of his own followers, the warrior Diarmuid. Finn and Grainne were betrothed and wed. But in her heart she secretly loved Diarmuid more than Finn, and on the night of the wedding feast she contrived a daring plan. First, she slipped a strong sleeping potion into everyone's drinks (except for Diarmuid's, of course) so that no one would interfere with her; then she revealed her love to Diarmuid and proposed that the two run away together. At first he refused. She was without doubt a beautiful woman, he said, and he had to confess that he did have strong feelings for her. But he was bound by his oath of loyalty to Finn, and

*Boann Ghulban, where, according to the prophecy, Diarmuid would be killed by the terrifying Boar of Boann Ghulban.*

honor dictated that he must not violate that oath. According to one account, Grainne shamed the warrior, saying that he was not man enough to become Finn's rival; another claims that the woman placed a magic spell on Diarmuid. Either way, he changed his mind and the two escaped and eloped.

When Finn woke up and realized that his wife and friend had betrayed him, he was both hurt and angry. He gathered together some of his best men and set out after the lovers, planning to punish them. It did not take long for the pursuers to catch up, and they surrounded Grainne and Diarmuid in a forest glade. Unluckily for Finn, Oenghus, god of love (who had many years before raised Diarmuid at the request of the

man's real father), intervened, whisking the lovers away to safety.

For the next seven years, Finn and the Fianna continued to pursue Grainne and Diarmuid. Then Oenghus negotiated a truce between Finn and his rival, which allowed the lovers to settle down and raise a family. However, the hero Finn still harbored a good deal of resentment for what had happened in the past, and he hoped that someday he might achieve vengeance. This hope was fulfilled during a great boar hunt. Finn found out about a prophecy that predicted that Diarmuid would be killed by the infamous and terrifying Boar of Boann Ghulban. So the leader of the Fianna invited Diarmuid to chase down the creature with him and some other warriors. Just as the prophecy had ordained, Diarmuid confronted the monster, which mortally wounded him. In this way, the honor of Finn and his heroes was satisfied at last. (It is said that Diarmuid, who was a hero in his own right, was later revived by his foster father, Oenghus, and that the two conversed happily every day in a dreamlike world beyond this one for many centuries thereafter.)

## Culhwch Wins the Fair Olwen

The concepts of love and honor were just as important to a hero who lived on the neighboring island of Britain a few hundred years after Finn got his revenge on Diarmuid. This Welsh champion was Culhwch, son of Cildydd, one of King Arthur's knights. Culhwch was also a cousin of Arthur, who ruled over the British kingdom of Camelot from his magnificent castle of the same name. Unfortunately for Culhwch, his mother died when he was very young; his father soon remarried, and this stepmother came to hate the boy. She placed a curse on him, saying that the only woman Culhwch would ever love and marry would be Olwen, daughter of Ysbaddaden. This was a terrible curse indeed, because Ysbaddaden was an extremely ornery one-eyed giant who would sooner die than allow his daughter to marry an ordinary man (though Olwen was herself an ordinary woman). Poor Culhwch was destined to spend his whole life pining away over a woman he could never have.

Culhwch grew to young manhood unaware of the curse that his stepmother

had inflicted on him. One day, however, on hearing Olwen's name for the first time, he fell madly in love with her (which was part of the curse); he decided that he must seek her out and marry her. His father suggested that he go to Camelot and ask for Arthur's assistance, which Culhwch did. Two of Arthur's knights, Cei and Bedwyr, agreed to accompany the young man on his quest for the hand of fair Olwen.

The three warriors journeyed overland for almost a year until they reached the towering castle in which Olwen and her monstrous father dwelled. The wife of a local shepherd arranged a meeting between Culhwch and Olwen, who, hearing that a handsome young suitor had arrived, slipped quietly out of the castle. Soon Culhwch gained his first glimpse of the woman of his dreams. According to the *Mabinogian*, an ancient Welsh romance:

> She arrived wearing a robe of flame-red silk about her, and around her neck a choker of red gold imbedded with precious pearls and rubies. . . . Whiter was her flesh than the foam of the wave. . . . Whiter were her breasts than the breast of the white swan. Redder were her cheeks than the reddest foxgloves. Who so beheld her would be filled with love for her. [53]

Culhwch proceeded to tell Olwen of his desire to marry her. And because she was immediately taken with the well-spoken young man, she accepted his proposal. However, she explained, her father was against any such marriage. So Culhwch must go to him and ask for her hand; and the knight must agree to perform any tasks the father demanded of him. Otherwise, she would not agree to the marriage.

Culhwch agreed to follow Olwen's instructions. But when he and his companions approached Ysbaddaden the next day, the giant flew into a rage and hurled spears at them. The men dodged the missiles and succeeded in hurling them back, wounding Ysbaddaden. The same thing occurred when the three men called on the giant the next day. On the third day, Ysbaddaden let loose his

spears again, and this time when Culhwch threw one back, it struck the giant in the eye. Ysbaddaden screamed and accused Culhwch of being a savage fellow. This was no way for a would-be son-in-law to treat a prospective father-in-law, the giant said.

Culhwch countered that it was the giant who had resorted to violence first and then loudly demanded Olwen's hand in marriage. To this, Ysbaddaden replied that he himself was the only one who could make demands in that land, and that if Culhwch wanted to marry his daughter, he must first complete a series of tasks. Only if all of these demands

*The Dolmen (burial chamber) of Diarmuid. Legend says Diarmuid was buried here before being revived by his foster father Oenghus.*

were met, and to the letter, would the giant grant his permission for the marriage.

Culhwch, who had no choice but to agree since he wanted Olwen more than life itself, found the tasks assigned by the giant extremely difficult and exhausting. There were thirty-nine of them; the most difficult and dangerous of all was to steal a comb, razor, and scissors from between the ears of Twrch Trwyth, a monstrous wild boar that roamed the forests of Ireland, and to return them to Ysbaddaden. King Arthur himself aided Culhwch in tracking Twrch Trwyth, a chase that took months and led them all over Ireland.

When all of the tasks had been completed, Culhwch and another knight, Goreu, went to Ysbaddaden. And as told in the ancient text:

> Culhwch asked, "Is your daughter mine now?" "She is," the giant answered. "But don't thank me for it. Instead, thank Arthur and his men, who won her for you. I would never have given in to you of my own free will." . . . Goreu suddenly caught Ysbaddaden by the hair and dragged him to a mound and cut off his head. . . . And that night Culhwch slept with Olwen and she was his only wife as long as he lived. [54]

## Gawain and the Green Knight

Another of Arthur's knights, Sir Gawain, also fought a giant of sorts in the form of the formidable Green Knight. One New Year's Eve, a huge man, dressed in green armor and wearing a green mask that hid most of his face, rode his horse, which was also green, right into Arthur's banquet hall at Camelot. Arthur demanded to know who the intruder was and what he wanted. In a deep, foreboding voice, the stranger said that he was the Green Knight and that he had come from the wastelands of northern Wales to issue a challenge. The knight produced a large ax and said that if any of Arthur's knights possessed the necessary courage, he could take the ax and attempt to cut off the Green Knight's head. At first Arthur and his followers simply stared in astonishment at the stranger. Why did they hesitate? the Green Knight asked. Were they men of courage, as they so often claimed to be, or just a pack of sniveling cowards?

Stung by this insult, Arthur sprang to his feet and rushed toward the horseman. But noble Gawain stopped him. Gawain begged the king to allow him to deal with this insolent fellow. Calming himself, the king agreed and Gawain approached the Green Knight, who held out the ax. Taking the weapon, Gawain prepared for battle, but his opponent simply dismounted and stood there, making no attempt to defend himself. Gawain commanded him to draw his sword. But the Green Knight still stood motionless. So Gawain raised the ax and without further ado he deftly severed the stranger's head in a single blow.

Seeing the head roll to the floor, Arthur, Gawain, and the others assumed the bizarre contest was over. But they were sorely mistaken. To their surprise, the Green Knight's torso remained upright, casually strode to its lost head, picked it up, and mounted the great green steed. The head's eyes looked at Gawain eerily and its lips moved, saying that if Gawain was not a coward, he would meet him at the Green Chapel in his homeland exactly one year from that day, there to continue the contest. Then the Green Knight turned and galloped away.

As a matter of honor, Gawain made the long journey to northern Wales and kept the fateful appointment. Three days before New Year's Eve, Gawain stopped to rest at a castle located only a few miles from the Green Chapel. The lord of the manor, Sir Bercilak, welcomed the traveler and bade him stay there the three days. During this interval, Gawain, a man of the purest honor and highest morals, found himself sorely tempted, for Sir Bercilak had an extremely beautiful wife. And each day the husband went out hunting and left Gawain and the wife alone together in the castle. For two days Gawain managed to resist the woman's considerable charms and her repeated offers of friendship, but on the third day he could resist no longer. When she offered a green sash as a token of friendship and love, out of courtesy he accepted.

The next day, which was New Year's Eve, Gawain made his way to the Green Chapel. And sure enough, the Green

## The Meeting at the Green Chapel

This is an excerpt from the long, anonymous medieval poem *Sir Gawain and the Green Knight* (quoted in Richard Barber's *The Arthurian Legends*). It begins with the Green Knight meeting Gawain at the Green Chapel and describes the first stroke of the ax.

*"Gawain," said the Green Knight, "may God guard you! . . . You have timed your travel here as a true man ought. You know plainly the pact we pledged between us. This time a twelvemonth ago, you took your portion [i.e., turn in the contest], and now at this New Year I should nimbly requite you [return the favor]. And we are here on our own in this valley, with no seconds to sunder us, spar as we will. Take your helmet off of your head and have your payment here. And offer no more argument or action than I did when you whipped off my head with one stroke." "No," said Gawain, "by God who gave me a soul, the grievous gash to come I grudge you not at all. Strike but the one stroke and I shall stand still and offer you no hindrance." . . . Head bent, Sir Gawain bowed, and showed his bright flesh bare. . . . Then the gallant in green quickly got ready, heaved his horrid weapon on high to hit Gawain . . . swinging it savagely enough to strike him dead. Had it driven down as direly as he aimed, the daring dauntless man would have died with the blow. . . . [But the Green Knight] suddenly stayed [halted] the descending ax.*

Knight was waiting there for him. Gawain dismounted and removed his helmet. He challenged the other man to strike at him, for Gawain was not afraid. If the Green Knight missed, Gawain would strike back and kill him. If, on the other hand, the Green Knight succeeded in parting Gawain's head from his body, so be it, for then the score would be even. However, the Green Knight neither missed nor parted Gawain's head. Instead, he stopped his ax a mere hair's breadth from Gawain's neck. The Green Knight explained that he had spared Gawain because during the first two days of his stay with Sir Bercilak, he had resisted his wife like an honorable man. Then the Green Knight raised the ax again and swung; this time the blade opened a small, shallow wound in Gawain's skin. The Green Knight said that he had shed some of the other man's blood because he had given in and accepted the green sash, expressing his feelings for another man's wife. However, this had obviously been more from courtesy than from lust or ill intent. So once more he had spared Gawain's life.

Gawain naturally wanted to know why the Green Knight was so concerned with the personal affairs of Sir Bercilak and his wife. The answer completely surprised Gawain. At that moment the Green Knight removed his

An *illuminated manuscript depicts Sir Gawain, who fought the Green Knight.*

helmet, revealing that he *was* Sir Bercilak! He told Gawain that he hoped the episode had taught him a lesson, namely, that, in the long run, moral purity is even more important than courtesy. Gawain agreed. And from that day forward, he always wore the green sash to remind himself of his momentary moral lapse. Indeed, as it had been for Cuchulainn, Finn MacCool, and other champions in that and other lands, maintaining one's honor and/or reputation at any cost was part of what made Gawain a hero for the ages.

# Native American Heroes: Shapers of the Habitable Earth

No single, universal set of myths and heroes exists for Native Americans as a group. This is because these peoples, popularly known as American Indians, did not belong to a single cultural unit with one widely accepted pantheon of gods and other mythical characters, as did the Greeks, Romans, and Chinese. Before and long after the appearance of Europeans in North America, the Native American peoples of the continent belonged to many separate groups and tribes that displayed a large, impressive, and rich cultural and religious diversity.

This diversity was based on various factors, perhaps the most important being the wide variation of geographical and physical settings in which these peoples lived. In the far north, for example, dwelled the Eskimo, or Inuit. Their world consisted mainly of seemingly endless and bleak expanses of ice and snow; so they had no settled agriculture and obtained their food, furs, and other products by hunting caribou, bears, seals, and other animals. In stark contrast, the Indians of the eastern Atlantic coast lived in more temperate, heavily forested lands. According to the late British Museum scholar Cottie Burland, these tribes

> were settled in semi-permanent villages by the time of the first European contact, and already possessed a basic farming culture that was more important than the hunting side of their economy. They had learned about maize [corn] agriculture from tribes to the south of them and had themselves established apple orchards and cared for many other vegetables including pumpkins and beans. Each village might

consist of 1,000 or more inhabitants living in bark-covered longhouses.[55]

There were many other Native American settings as well, of course, including the thick forests and swamplands and humid climate of the American Southeast; the rolling plains of the Midwest on which roamed vast herds of buffalo; and the hot, dry deserts of the Southwest, where the people often constructed their homes from sun-baked mud.

The upshot of this wide variety of settings was that separate tribes or regional groups of tribes developed distinctive religious views, gods, and myths; and the nature of the heroes, monsters, and events of these myths were heavily colored by their local settings. The Inuit living near the Bering Sea (in northern Canada), for instance, believed that one of the major predators of that region, the killer whale, could transform itself into a wolf. In that form it supposedly roamed the icy tundra looking for people to eat. On the other hand, the myths of the Cheyenne, who lived on the Great Plains, were often very different. Their lives revolved around the hunting of buffalo; and one of their heroes, Falling Star, was famous for killing a white crow that flew ahead of human hunters and warned the buffalo to flee.

Still, when viewed overall, most (although certainly not all) Native American mythologies do have a few basic themes in common, even if the local details are usually very different. "In the continent as a whole," says former University of Nebraska scholar Hartley Alexander,

> there is a generally definable scheme within which the mythic conceptions of the North American [Indian] fall into place. . . . There is a world above, the home of the Sky Father and the celestial powers; there is the world below, the embodiment of the Earth Mother and the abode of the dead; [and] there is the central

*A killer whale totem. The Inuit believed the killer whale could transform itself into a wolf.*

plain of the earth. . . . A few tribes recognize a creator who . . . generates the world and its inhabitants; but the usual conception is either of a pre-existent sky-world . . . or else of a kind of cosmic womb from which the first people had their origin. . . . The next act of the world drama details the deeds of a hero or of twin heroes who are the shapers and law-givers of the habitable earth. They conquer the primitive monsters and . . . generally one of them is slain and passes to the underworld to become its lord. The theft of fire, the origin of death, the liberation of the animals, [and] the giving of the arts . . . are all themes that recur once and again.[56]

The three Native American heroic myths that follow illustrate some of these overriding themes. Lone Man and Hiawatha are shapers of civilization; and the story of the young man and the daughter of Thunder is a variation of the myth of the theft of fire, which also illustrates the pervasive image (one seen around the world) of the hero as monster-slayer.

## Lone Man Reduces Human Suffering

Lone Man's story was told among the Mandan, a tribe that lived along the Missouri River in the American Midwest. Long, long ago, as the tribal elders told it, the world was covered with water and Lone Man walked on the surface of the waters. Suddenly he met up with another person, who called

*The story of Lone Man, who transformed himself into a human in order to help the Indians, was told by the Mandan tribe, shown fishing in the Missouri River.*

himself First Man. After they had introduced themselves, First Man asked Lone Man where he had come from. Also, who were his parents? Lone Man was perplexed and tried hard to remember. But he could not. He said that in truth he did not know exactly where he had come from. All he knew was that he was there. First Man smiled and explained how it was the same with him. But since somehow they did exist, it made sense for them to create a more hospitable environment, one in which they could make homes for themselves. For that, they would need to make some land in the midst of all this water.

Lone Man agreed with this idea. The two continued to walk along the water's surface until they spied a duck paddling along. They instructed the duck to dive down to the bottom of the ocean and bring up some earth, and the duck did so. It repeated this process three more times, so that there were four pieces of earth, which Lone Man and First Man now used to create land, from which the first grass and trees began to grow. Before long there were mountains, plains, valleys, streams, ponds, and so forth as far as the eye could see. Next Lone Man and his companion fashioned buffalo, deer, cattle, sheep, and other animals to populate the land.

Several years passed. And then the two superhuman beings stumbled onto a pleasant surprise. They found human tribes living on the land, attempting to eke out their livings by hunting, fishing, and growing corn. First Man and Lone Man had no more idea of where the humans had come from than

they had of where they themselves had come from. Fascinated, Lone Man began to observe one of these tribes, the Mandan, while First Man said good-bye and journeyed on toward the west.

After watching the Mandan for several seasons, Lone Man saw that sometimes, no matter how hard they struggled, they suffered from hunger and other deprivations. Because his heart was as large as his physical strength (which was considerable), he took pity on them. He wanted to share in their struggle and to make their lives easier by showing them better ways of doing some things. And the best way to do this, he decided, was to become a human.

There are different versions of how Lone Man accomplished this crucial transformation. One says that he shrank himself down and entered a kernel of corn; and when a young woman ate the kernel she became pregnant and gave birth to Lone Man in human form. Another version of the story claims that Lone Man took the form of a dead buffalo floating in a stream. A young girl came along and ate some buffalo meat, which caused her to become pregnant and give birth to Lone Man.

However it was that he became human, Lone Man grew into a remarkably handsome and popular young man. He showed the people how to make warmer and more beautiful clothes. He also demonstrated new and more effective ways of finding and trapping animals, so that the people had more to eat and famine became rare. In addition, Lone Man became a peacemaker. Whenever members of the tribe quarreled

# The Natural Was Inseparable from the Supernatural

The nature and great diversity of Native American religion, which shaped and colored the characters and events of Indian myths, is summarized clearly in this excerpt from Carl Waldman's highly informative *Atlas of the North American Indian.*

*Indians were an especially . . . reverent people, viewing themselves as extensions of animate and inanimate nature. Religion and ritual were a function of all activity—the food quest and other survival-related work, technology, social and political organization, warfare, and art. Religion and magic were fused with practical science—for example, prayer was used in conjunction with practical hunting and fishing techniques, and incantations [chants that cast spells] accompanied effective herbal remedies in the curing of disease. For Indians, the natural was inseparable from the supernatural. Myth was a way of understanding reality. Religion played a prominent role in the interpretation of the universe and in the adaptation of human activity to the patterns of nature. . . . Indian religion presents a wondrous variety of beliefs, sacraments, and systems. Different tribes or related groups of peoples had different views of the supernatural world, with varying types of deities and spirits . . . ghosts, or the spirits of dead ancestors; animal and plant spirits; spirits of natural phenomena, such as sun or rain gods; benevolent or guardian spirits . . . and malevolent [evil] demons. . . . Along with these diverse types of supernatural beings, Indian peoples had variegated [differing] mythologies and lore concerning the creation and structure of the universe; an array of rites, ceremonies, and sacred objects; and differing systems of religious organization.*

A Blackfoot Native American man raises his arms in prayer.

with one another or with people of neighboring tribes, he stepped in and mediated, showing that war and violence might sometimes be avoided using common sense and compassion.

Eventually Lone Man faced his greatest test. A powerful and malicious being named Maninga arrived on the scene and attempted to destroy Lone Man and his people by transforming itself into a great flood. As Burland tells it:

> At this time there were five Mandan villages full of people, and as the flood came higher the villages were abandoned one by one. Lone Man led his people to the last village. There he planted a sacred cedar tree.... Then he built a small stockade of willow planks. It was called the Great Canoe, though it never floated. As the flood grew, it lapped the sides of the Great Canoe.[57]

Luckily, Lone Man was smarter than Maninga and tricked the being into making the waters recede.

A few years after this incident, Lone Man came to feel that his work was done and that it was time for him to move on. One day he packed his things and said farewell to the Mandan, who were exceedingly sad to see him go. Then he departed and disappeared over the western horizon. According to Burland, "Some of the stockade that the Indians believed to be the remains of the Great Canoe can still be seen

An Ojibwa tribesman poses as Hiawatha, a real person who, by the 1700s, had become a mythological hero.

at the old Mandan village on the left bank of the Upper Missouri."[58]

## The Power of the Message of Peace

The myth of another peacemaker and champion of civilized life recalls the deeds of an actual historical figure—Hiawatha. The real Hiawatha lived in the 1500s. His deeds were so great that by the time white Europeans heard about him some two centuries later, he had achieved the status of a mythological hero. (The famous poem *The Song of Hiawatha*, by Henry Wadsworth Longfellow, deals with a character that was different in many ways than the real Hiawatha.) Hiawatha's principal achievement was to unite the five Iroquois tribes—the Seneca, Cayuga, Onondaga, Oneida, and Mohawk—who had long been at war with one another, into a peaceful, productive federation of equals.

According to the legend, year after year the warriors of the five Iroquois nations raided one another's villages. On a typical raid they would swoop down on the enemy, screaming frightening war cries and swinging tomahawks and clubs left and right. They would burn lodges, killing the occupants or taking them prisoner; often the captives were later tortured to death. This destructive cycle of hatred, killing, and revenge became so commonplace that many Iroquois assumed it was the natural way of things and would therefore go on forever.

However, one of the Oneida, whose name was Deganawidah, saw it differently. He was a prophet who had the magical ability to see into the future. And he predicted that in his own lifetime a great hero would arise and unite the five warring tribes into a friendly brotherhood. Most people scoffed at this notion. But soon the prophecy began to be fulfilled; for a chief of the Onondaga (some accounts say the Mohawk)—Hiawatha—had the intelligence and moral sense to envision peace and the courage and political skills to fight for it. He began by proposing his great idea to the elders of his own tribe. His main opponent was the tribal magician, Atotarho, who was so filled with hate that he wanted the wars to continue. Most elders were afraid to disagree with Atotarho. The reason was that when he grew angry, his hair turned into

a mass of twisting serpents and his gaze could make people drop dead in their tracks. Because he was a magician, Atotarho could also make animals do his evil bidding. When Hiawatha pleaded his peace plan before the elders a second time, the magician summoned a huge white bird, which knocked down and killed Hiawatha's daughter.

Humiliated and grief-stricken, Hiawatha took leave of his tribe and journeyed to the main village of the Oneida. There, he met Deganawidah, who, because he could see into the future, had been expecting him. It did his heart good, Deganawidah said, that a man of Hiawatha's greatness had finally arisen in their midst. The prophet declared that he would help Hiawatha present his extraordinary ideas to the leaders of the tribe. Indeed, Deganawidah stood beside Hiawatha that very night at the Oneida council fire, where the elders were so impressed that they became the first of the five tribes to agree to the plan. In the months that followed, Hiawatha delivered a series of magnificent, impassioned speeches to the councils of the other tribes; and they too agreed to set aside their ancient grudges and give peace a chance.

Only Hiawatha's own tribe—the Onondaga—still held out, mainly because of the influence of Atotarho. At this point Hiawatha had so much backing, both inside and outside of the tribe, that he could have killed his opponent and no one would have considered him a murderer. However, Hiawatha maintained that there had been enough killing. Instead, he stood before Atotarho and delivered the most moving speech of his life; it was so moving, in fact, that the magician could no longer resist the compelling power of the message of peace and he came to agree with Hiawatha. The legend claims that Hiawatha combed the serpents out of Atotarho's hair. Although this aspect of the story is obviously mythical, there is no doubt that the five nations were united, and future generations of Iroquois remembered Hiawatha as their greatest hero.

## Pursuing the Daughter of Thunder

While the myths of Lone Man and Hiawatha concern heroes who directly shaped or saved civilization, the myth of another Native American hero concerns an act that

*Native Americans often used petroglyphs (rock drawings) to tell the stories of Lone Man, Hiawatha, and other mythical heroes.*

# A Legendary Indian's Contribution to American Government

The unification of the Iroquois tribes into a democratic political federation, an accomplishment attributed to the legendary Hiawatha, had an indirect influence on the early development of the U.S. government. After the American Revolution, the new American government operated under rules called the Articles of Confederation. But these rules proved inadequate to run the swiftly growing nation and the founding fathers searched for a better system. They looked at European models, such as the histories of the governments and legal systems of Britain and ancient Athens, of course; and in addition, they observed the Iroquois federation. Thomas Jefferson, Benjamin Franklin, and other American leaders noted that the five Iroquois tribes (or nations)—the Mohawk, Onondaga, Oneida, Seneca, and Cayuga—worked together much like a republican nation made up of individual states. Each tribe sent delegates to regular meetings of a Grand Council representing all the tribes. According to the modern Seneca scholar John C. Mohawk (in an article in Frederick Hoxie's Encyclopedia of North American Indians), the federation's Grand Council "was empowered to treat with foreign nations and peoples and to settle disputes among the Five Nations. The Iroquois Confederacy is divided into houses . . . in structure similar to that found in upper and lower houses in some parliamentary systems [like that of Britain]." The Iroquois political system greatly impressed Jefferson

*America's founding fathers modeled the new nation's government, in part, after the Iroquois Federation.*

and his colleagues, who went on to combine some Iroquois concepts with others from Europe and some new ideas of their own. The result was the U.S. Constitution, ratified in 1789 and considered one of the greatest political documents in history. Unfortunately, neither the Iroquois nor Hiawatha received any credit or recognition for their innovative approach to government at the time, and only in recent years have scholars come to appreciate the contribution Native Americans made to America's government.

made civilization possible. Far to the west of the Iroquois homeland, in what is now Northern California, lived the Maidu tribe. The Maidu preserved the memory of their own heroes, one of the most important of whom was a strong, resourceful young man who secured dependable sources of light and fire for the people. Because his name has been lost in the mists of time, let us call him the Hero.

In the bygone days when the Hero was growing up, the legends say, "the world was dark and there was no fire; the only light was the Morning, and it was so far away in the high mountains of the east that the people could not see it; they lived in total darkness."[59] There was one exception to this rather grim state of affairs. Every now and then, when the great spirit Thunder roared on high, bolts of lightning zigzagged through the sky, illuminating the world for a few brief seconds. Sometimes the lightning would ignite a small fire, but the flames would quickly dissipate and extinguish themselves, plunging the land back into darkness. The people traditionally believed that these brilliant flashes of light were the daughters of Thunder.

One day the Hero was out looking for food with his younger brother. Suddenly there was a bright flash of light, and they saw that one of Thunder's daughters was floating in the air nearby. Her features were illuminated in a radiant white light, and it was plain to the young men that she was very beautiful. The Hero found himself overcome with desire for her. So he asked her not to go away, but instead to stay and become

his wife, in return for which he would do his best to make her happy. The shining girl answered that he appeared to be a fine and capable young warrior, one that a woman would be proud to call a husband. But first he must prove himself worthy. He should pursue her. And if he could overcome the obstacles her father placed in his path, she would be allowed to marry him. As if to confirm and seal this strange bargain, a loud crack of thunder echoed across the land.

The Hero immediately began pursuing Thunder's daughter, who streaked through the air ahead of him. Before long he found his path blocked by a vast briar field with thorns so large and sharp that he would be torn to pieces if he tried to cross it. Thinking quickly, he removed a piece of flint from the pouch he wore around his waist. After sharpening the edge of the flint against some rocks, he began cutting his way through the briars, and in less than an hour he emerged on the far side of the field. Thunder's daughter seemed pleasantly surprised at the young man's resourcefulness. But she continued her flight, and soon she led the Hero to a meadow filled with deadly rattlesnakes. Once more he used his wits, this time fashioning moccasins out of slabs of rock and crossing the meadow wearing these protective shoes, which the snakes' fangs could not penetrate.

These were only the first of many obstacles that Thunder created to block the Hero's pursuit of his daughter. The valiant young man managed to safely cross a frozen lake riddled with patches of thin ice, which might have given way if he had stepped on them;

avoided eating some poisoned food left along the path by Thunder; escaped the clutches of a fearsome water beast that attacked him when he was attempting to cross a river; slew a huge grizzly bear that pursued him by order of Thunder; and used his bow and arrow to kill one of Thunder's deer, which was vulnerable in only one tiny spot on its body.

Eventually, having overcome all of the obstacles placed before him, the Hero reached Thunder's great lodge at the far edge of the world. Thunder, who was obviously surprised and impressed, said that the young man had done well. So he would keep his side of the bargain and let the Hero marry his daughter. Proudly, the Hero took his new bride back to his homeland; and she not only brought him great happiness, but also provided his people with light to dispel the darkness and fire for warmth and cooking.

# Notes

## Introduction: Halfway Between Gods and Humans

1. Michael Grant, *Myths of the Greeks and Romans*. New York: New American Library, 1962, pp. 45–46.
2. Joseph Campbell, *The Hero with a Thousand Faces*. Princeton: Princeton University Press, 1968, p. 30.
3. Dorothy Norman, *The Hero: Myth/Image/Symbol*. New York: World, 1969, p. 4.

## Chapter 1: Mesopotamian Heroes: The Search for Immortality

4. John Gray, *Near Eastern Mythology*. New York: Peter Bedrick Books, 1982, p. 26.
5. Quoted in Stephanie Dalley, trans., *Myths from Mesopotamia*. New York: Oxford University Press, 1989, p. 18.
6. Quoted in Dalley, *Myths from Mesopotamia*, p. 112.
7. Quoted in Dalley, *Myths from Mesopotamia*, pp. 113–14.
8. Quoted in Dalley, *Myths from Mesopotamia*, pp. 52–53.
9. Quoted in Dalley, *Myths from Mesopotamia*, pp. 92–93.
10. Quoted in Dalley, *Myths from Mesopotamia*, pp. 185–86.

## Chapter 2: Greek Heroes: Valiant Warriors in a Golden Age

11. Quoted in Rhoda A. Hendricks, trans., *Classical Gods and Heroes: Myths as Told by the Ancient Authors*. New York: Morrow Quill, 1974, p. 170.
12. Plutarch, *Life of Theseus*, in *The Rise and Fall of Athens: Nine Greek Lives by Plutarch*. Trans. Ian Scott-Kilvert. New York: Penguin, 1960, p. 24.
13. Quoted in Hendricks, *Classical Gods and Heroes*, p. 172.

14. Edith Hamilton, *Mythology*. New York: New American Library, 1940, p. 161.
15. Quoted in Hendricks, *Classical Gods and Heroes*, p. 157.
16. Quoted in Hendricks, *Classical Gods and Heroes*, p. 159.
17. Homer, *Iliad*. Trans. Robert Fagles. New York: Penguin Books, 1990, pp. 407–408.
18. Homer, *Iliad*, trans. Fagles, p. 410.
19. Homer, *Iliad*, trans. Fagles, p. 413.
20. Homer, *Iliad*, trans. Fagles, pp. 545–46.
21. Homer, *Iliad*, trans. Fagles, p. 550.
22. Homer, *Iliad*, trans. Fagles, p. 551.
23. Homer, *Iliad*, trans. Fagles, p. 552.

## Chapter 3—Roman Heroes: Founders of the Eternal City

24. T. J. Cornell, *The Beginnings of Rome: Italy and Rome from the Bronze Age to the Punic Wars (c.1000–264 B.C.)*. London: Routledge, 1995, p. 65.
25. Virgil, *The Aeneid*. Trans. Patric Dickinson. New York: New American Library, 1961, p. 9.
26. Virgil, *Aeneid*, p. 75.
27. Virgil, *Aeneid*, pp. 57–58.
28. Virgil, *Aeneid*, p. 82.
29. Virgil, *Aeneid*, pp. 83–85.
30. Virgil, *Aeneid*, pp. 141–42.
31. Virgil, *Aeneid*, p. 14.
32. Livy, *The History of Rome from Its Foundation*. Books 1–5 published as *Livy: The Early History of Rome*. Trans. Aubrey de Sélincourt. New York: Penguin, 1971, pp. 39–40.
33. Plutarch, *Life of Romulus*, in *Parallel Lives*, published as *Lives of the Noble Grecians and Romans*. Trans. John Dryden. New York: Random House, 1932, p. 31.
34. Livy, *History of Rome*, pp. 42–43.
35. Livy, *History of Rome*, p. 115.

36. Livy, *History of Rome*, p. 116.
37. Livy, *History of Rome*, p. 216.

## Chapter 4: Chinese Heroes: Struggling to Survive in a Hostile World

38. Quoted in Anthony Christie, *Chinese Mythology*. New York: Peter Bedrick Books, 1985, pp. 41–42.
39. Derk Bodde, "Myths of Ancient China," in *Mythologies of the Ancient World*. Ed. Samuel N. Kramer. Garden City, NY: Doubleday, 1961, p. 375.
40. Bodde, "Myths of Ancient China," p. 375.
41. Quoted in Bodde, "Myths of Ancient China," p. 399.
42. Quoted in Anne Birrell, *Chinese Mythology: An Introduction*. Baltimore: Johns Hopkins University Press, 1993, p. 80.
43. Quoted in Birrell, *Chinese Mythology*, p. 147.
44. Quoted in Bodde, "Myths of Ancient China," p. 400.
45. Quoted in Birrell, *Chinese Mythology*, p. 180.
46. Quoted in Birrell, *Chinese Mythology*, p. 180.

## Chapter 5: Celtic Heroes: Feasting and Fighting in an Ideal World

47. Miranda J. Green, *Celtic Myths*. Austin: University of Texas Press, 1993, p. 8.
48. Peter B. Ellis, *The Celtic Empire: The First Millennium of Celtic History, c.1000 B.C.–51 A.D.* Durham, NC: Carolina Academic Press, 1990, pp. 16–17.
49. Quoted in Arthur Cotterell, *Celtic Mythology*. New York: Lorenz Books, 1998, p. 34.
50. Cotterell, *Celtic Mythology*, p. 34.
51. Quoted in Green, *Celtic Myths*, p. 26.
52. Proinsias Mac Cana, *Celtic Mythology*. New York: Peter Bedrick Books, 1985, pp. 104–105.
53. Quoted in Richard Barber, ed., *The Arthurian Legends: An Illustrated Anthology*. New York: Peter Bedrick Books, 1979, p. 36.
54. Quoted in Barber, *Arthurian Legends*, p. 43.

## Chapter 6: Native American Heroes: Shapers of the Habitable Earth

55. Cottie Burland, *North American Indian Mythology*. Rev. Marion Wood. New York: Peter Bedrick Books, 1985, p. 9.
56. Hartley B. Alexander, *The Mythology of All Races, Volume X: North American*. New York: Cooper Square, 1964, pp. xxiii–xxiv.
57. Burland, *North American Indian Mythology*, p. 84.
58. Burland, *North American Indian Mythology*, p. 84.
59. Quoted in Alexander, *Mythology of All Races*, p. 230.

# For Further Reading

David Bellingham, *An Introduction to Greek Mythology*. Secaucus, NJ: Chartwell Books, 1989. Explains the major Greek myths and legends and their importance to the ancient Greeks. Contains many beautiful photos and drawings.

Peter Connolly, *The Legend of Odysseus*. New York: Oxford University Press, 1986. An excellent, easy-to-read summary of the events of Homer's *Iliad* and *Odyssey*, including many informative sidebars about the way people lived in Mycenaean times. Also contains many stunning illustrations re-creating the fortresses, homes, ships, and armor of the period.

Arthur Cotterell, *Celtic Mythology*. New York: Lorenz Books, 1998. This first-rate introductory mythology book features an encyclopedia-style, alphabetical listing of mythical characters, supported by many beautiful color illustrations. Highly recommended.

Richard Erdoes and Alfonso Ortiz, eds., *American Indian Myths and Legends*. New York: Pantheon Books, 1985. Dozens of entertaining Native American tales are included in this well-written volume.

Charles Kingsley, *The Heroes*. Santa Rosa, CA: Classics Press, 1968. This is a reprint of the original book by Kingsley—the renowned nineteenth-century social reformer, university professor, and classical scholar—a work he wrote for his three children. Contains his superb retellings of the stories of Jason, Perseus, Theseus, and Heracles.

Don Nardo, ed., *Readings on Homer*. San Diego: Greenhaven Press, 1998. This useful volume contains several somewhat scholarly yet readable essays about various aspects of the *Iliad* and *Odyssey*, as well as about Homer's style and impact, each essay by a noted expert in the classics.

Neil Philip, *The Illustrated Book of Myths: Tales and Legends of the World*. New York: Dorling Kindersley, 1995. An excellent introduction to world mythology for young people, enlivened with many stunning photos and drawings.

———, *Mythology*. New York: Knopf, 1999. Another fine beginners' mythology volume by Philip, who has written a number of other children's books on the subject, including *Fairy Tales of Eastern Europe* and *The Arabian Nights*.

Tao Tao Liu Sanders and Johnny Pau, *Dragons, Gods, and Spirits from Chinese Mythology*. New York: Peter Bedrick Books, 1994. This beautifully mounted book, featuring numerous colorful drawings, has a nicely written text that introduces the characters and situations of many of the important Chinese myths.

# Major Works Consulted

Anne Birrell, *Chinese Mythology: An Introduction*. Baltimore: Johns Hopkins University Press, 1993. An informative, somewhat scholarly volume that contains about three hundred mythological narratives taken from classical Chinese mythology, some never before published in English.

Thomas Bulfinch, *Bulfinch's Mythology*. New York: Dell, 1959. This is one of several versions of this well-known and useful work, which is itself a modern compilation of two of Bulfinch's original books—*The Age of Fable* (1855), a retelling of the Greek and Roman myths, and *The Age of Chivalry* (1858), an account of the Arthurian legends.

Cottie Burland, *North American Indian Mythology*. Rev. Marion Wood. New York: Peter Bedrick Books, 1985. This volume, by the late Cottie Burland—who was a scholar at the British Museum and an authority on Native American myths—is divided according to geographical regions, such as "Hunters of the Northern Forests," "Farmers of the Eastern Woodlands," and "Dwellers on the Mesas."

Proinsias Mac Cana, *Celtic Mythology*. New York: Peter Bedrick Books, 1985. A well-organized and informative description of Celtic folklore, including some of the tales of Arthur and the other traditional heroes of yore.

Michael Grant, *Myths of the Greeks and Romans*. New York: New American Library, 1962. One of the twentieth century's most prolific and respected classical historians here delivers a fine rendition of the important Greek and Roman myths, along with plenty of background information and analysis.

Edith Hamilton, *Mythology*. New York: New American Library, 1940. Hamilton's excellent retelling of the Greek myths is still considered by many to be the best and most entertaining overview of its kind.

Rhoda A. Hendricks, trans., *Classical Gods and Heroes: Myths as Told by the Ancient Authors*. New York: Morrow Quill, 1974. A collection of easy-to-read translations of famous Greek myths and tales, as told by ancient Greek and Romans writers, including Homer, Hesiod, Pindar, Apollodorus, Ovid, and Virgil.

Homer, *Iliad*. Trans. Robert Fagles. New York: Penguin Books, 1990; also trans. E. V. Rieu. Baltimore: Penguin Books, 1950. These are two of the best translations of Homer's great epic about the Trojan War, the first and still one of the greatest examples of Western literature. For substantial synopses of the *Iliad* in English, I recommend Connolly's *The Legend of Odysseus*, Grant's *Myths of the Greeks and Romans*, Hamilton's *Mythology* (all three, see above), and Morford and Lenardon's *Classical Mythology* (see below).

Livy, *The History of Rome from Its Foundation*. Books 1–5 published as *Livy: The Early History of Rome*. Trans. Aubrey de Sélincourt. New York: Penguin, 1971. An excellent translation of these parts of Livy's massive and masterful history, written during Rome's golden literary age of the late first century B.C. Contains the most extensive available primary source descriptions of Romulus and the Roman foundation.

Stewart Perowne, *Roman Mythology*. London: Paul Hamlyn, 1969. This volume by Perowne—the noted historian, archaeologist, and author of several important works about Rome—is well written and nicely illustrated.

Virgil, *The Aeneid*. Trans. Patric Dickinson. New York: New American Library, 1961. An excellent translation of the epic poem that constitutes the single major source for the legends of the Roman founder Aeneas.

Philip Wilkinson, *The Illustrated Dictionary of Mythology*. New York: Dorling Kindersley, 1998. This well-written, handsomely mounted book contains short overviews of hundreds of mythological characters, facts, and stories of peoples from around the world.

Michael Wood, *In Search of the Trojan War*. New York: New American Library, 1985. An extremely well written and entertaining examination of the myth of the Trojan War and how German archaeologist Heinrich Schliemann and other scholars proved that the legend was based on fact.

# Additional Works Consulted

Hartley B. Alexander, *The Mythology of All Races, Volume X: North American.* New York: Cooper Square, 1964.

Richard Barber, ed., *The Arthurian Legends: An Illustrated Anthology.* New York: Peter Bedrick Books, 1979.

Derk Bodde, "Myths of Ancient China," in *Mythologies of the Ancient World.* Ed. Samuel N. Kramer. Garden City, NY: Doubleday, 1961.

C. M. Bowra, *The Greek Experience.* New York: New American Library, 1957.

Joseph Campbell, *The Hero with a Thousand Faces.* Princeton: Princeton University Press, 1968.

———, *Myths to Live By.* New York: Bantam Books, 1972.

Rodney Castleden, *Minoans: Life in Bronze Age Crete.* New York: Routledge, 1993.

C. W. Ceram, *Hands on the Past: Pioneer Archaeologists Tell Their Own Story.* New York: Knopf, 1966.

Nora K. Chadwick and Barry Cunliffe, *The Celts.* New York: Penguin, 1998.

Anthony Christie, *Chinese Mythology.* New York: Peter Bedrick Books, 1985.

T. J. Cornell, *The Beginnings of Rome: Italy and Rome from the Bronze Age to the Punic Wars (c.1000–264 B.C.).* London: Routledge, 1995.

Stephanie Dalley, trans., *Myths from Mesopotamia.* New York: Oxford University Press, 1989.

Patricia B. Ebrey, *The Cambridge Illustrated History of China.* New York: Cambridge University Press, 1996.

Peter B. Ellis, *The Celtic Empire: The First Millennium of Celtic History, c.1000 B.C.–51 A.D.* Durham, NC: Carolina Academic Press, 1990.

Charles Freeman, *The Greek Achievement: The Foundation of the Western World.* New York: Viking/Penguin, 1999.

Jane F. Gardner, *Roman Myths.* Austin: University of Texas Press, 1993.

L. Carrington Goodrich, *A Short History of the Chinese People.* New York: Harper and Row, 1963.

Norma L. Goodrich, *Ancient Myths.* New York: New American Library, 1960.

John Gray, *Near Eastern Mythology.* New York: Peter Bedrick Books, 1982.

Miranda J. Green, *Celtic Myths.* Austin: University of Texas Press, 1993.

Frederick E. Hoxie, ed., *Encyclopedia of North American Indians.* New York: Houghton Mifflin, 1996.

Samuel N. Kramer, *Cradle of Civilization.* New York: Time-Life, 1967.

———, ed., *Mythologies of the Ancient World.* Garden City, NY: Doubleday, 1961.

Dean A. Miller, *The Epic Hero.* Baltimore: John Hopkins University Press, 2000.

Mark P. O. Morford and Robert J. Lenardon, *Classical Mythology.* New York: Longman, 1985.

Dorothy Norman, *The Hero: Myth/Image/Symbol.* New York: World, 1969.

R. M. Ogilvie, *The Romans and Their Gods in the Age of Augustus.* New York: W. W. Norton, 1969.

John G. Pedley, *Greek Art and Archaeology.* New York: Harry N. Abrams, 1993.

John Pinsent, *Greek Mythology*. New York: Peter Bedrick Books, 1986.

Plutarch, *Life of Theseus*, in *The Rise and Fall of Athens: Nine Greek Lives by Plutarch*. Trans. Ian Scott-Kilvert. New York: Penguin, 1960.

————, *Parallel Lives*, published as *Lives of the Noble Grecians and Romans*. Trans. John Dryden. New York: Random House, 1932.

James B. Pritchard, ed., *Ancient Near Eastern Texts Relating to the Old Testament*. Princeton: Princeton University Press, 1969.

W. H. D. Rouse, *Gods, Heroes and Men of Ancient Greece*. New York: New American Library, 1957.

H. W. F. Saggs, *Civilization Before Greece and Rome*. New Haven: Yale University Press, 1989.

M. S. Silk, *Homer: The Iliad*. Cambridge, Eng.: Cambridge University Press, 1987.

Carl Waldman, *Atlas of the North American Indian*. New York: Facts On File, 1985.

# Index

# Picture Credits

Cover Photo: © Archivo Iconografico, S.A./Corbis

Art Archive, 59

Art Resource/Erich Lessing, 20, 29

Art Resource, NY/Pierpont Morgan Library, 85

Art Resource, NY/Scala, 34

Bettmann/Corbis, 9, 40, 48, 51, 52, 90

Bridgeman Art Library, 54

Ric Ergenbright/Corbis, 64

Historic Picture Archive/Corbis, 33, 35, 37

Aralado de Luca/Corbis, 31

Buddy Mays/Corbis, 32

Michael Maslan Historic Photographs/Corbis, 87

Dego Lezama Orezzoli/Corbis, 12

Giann Dagli Orti/Corbis, 19

Bill Ross/Corbis, 93

Nic Wheeler/Corbis, 17

Roger Wood/ Corbis, 44

John T. Young/Corbis, 68

Heck's Pictorial Archive of Art and Architecture, 55

Hulton Deutsch Collection/Corbis, 91

Irish Picture Library, 78, 80, 82

Library of Congress, 88

Mary Evans Picture Library, 63, 74, 77

Northwind Picture Archives, 15, 27, 45, 94

# About the Author

Historian Don Nardo has written several volumes about ancient cultures and their religious beliefs and mythologies, among them *Life in Ancient Athens*, *The Persian Empire*, *Greek and Roman Mythology*, and *Egyptian Mythology*. Mr. Nardo is also the editor of Greenhaven Press's massive *Greenhaven Encyclopedia of Greek and Roman Mythology*. He lives with his wife, Christine, in Massachusetts.